DAILY GUIDEBOOK

BASED ON THE EPIC TV MINISERIES

THE BIBLE

30-DAY EXPERIENCE

WRITTEN BY BOB HOSTETLER

The Bible 30-Day Experience GuideBook
Copyright © 2013 by Outreach, Inc.

Published by Outreach, Inc. under license from Hachette Book Group, Inc., New York, NY, and in conjunction with Lightworkers Media and Hearst Productions, Inc.

Photographs used by permission of Lightworkers Media and Hearst Productions, Inc.

Outreach, Inc. Colorado Springs, CO 80919
www.outreach.com

ISBN: 978-1-935541-69-1

Written by: Bob Hostetler
Cover Design: Tim Downs
Interior Design: Tim Downs
Edited by: Dave Bordon
Printed in the United States of America

CONTENTS

INTRODUCTION

WHAT IS *THE BIBLE 30-DAY EXPERIENCE?*

The Bible 30-Day Experience GuideBook is a five-week study to help you experience the life-changing stories, characters, and principles in the Bible like never before! Based on the epic TV miniseries, *The Bible*, this five-week study will help you experience the Bible in a whole new way.

The Bible 30-Day Experience GuideBook is designed to correspond and work with The Bible 30-Day Experience DVD Study by teaching you more than just some good lessons. It has the potential to change your life. It was written to help you experience the truth of God's Word and is intended to give you insights regarding your relationship with God—insights that can bear fruit in your life and last for eternity.

The thirty daily lessons and readings included in this volume are designed to help you understand how much God wants to have a relationship with you. These stories reveal God's intentions toward each of us—His hopes and dreams—and our opportunity and potential. Each lesson in this guidebook shows how Jesus is foreshadowed in the great stories of the Old Testatment and is the scarlet thread of redemption promised from Genesis to Revelation. There are five overarching themes covered:

- **From Death to Life:** God's plan of redemption, revealed over and over again in the stories and commands of Scriptures, is to provide a way for sinful, mortal human beings to be delivered from certain death and given a new and abundant life. As Jesus said, "Whoever hears my word and believes him who sent me has eternal life and will not be judged but has crossed over from death to life" (John 5:24).
- **From Slavery to Freedom:** Like the children of Israel fleeing Egypt, when a human soul experiences God's redemption, he or she is released from captivity and blessed with true and lasting freedom. Jesus put it like this: "You will know the truth, and the truth will set you free" (John 8:32).
- **From Victim to Victor:** The soul that has experienced God's

saving power also experiences a new reality. No longer is such a man or woman a victim of sin and circumstance, because in everything, God has promised: "When you pass through the waters, I will be with you; and when you pass through the rivers, they will not sweep over you. When you walk through the fire, you will not be burned; the flames will not set you ablaze" (Isaiah 43:2).

- **From Religion to Relationship:** God's redemptive purpose is not the establishment of a religion but rather the enjoyment of a relationship, a covenant of love, a living and thriving relationship with Jesus. As John the beloved disciple wrote, "We live in him and he in us" (1 John 4:13); and that relationship meets needs and accomplishes things that no amount of religion could ever do.

- **From Darkness to Light:** When God saves a human soul, he delivers that person from the darkness of confusion, fear, and doubt, and bestows the light of a new purpose, peace, and presence in that person's life—"out of darkness into his marvelous light" (1 Peter 2:9, ESV).

There are also small-group and individual study and discussion questions to help you go deeper in the daily lessons and readings found in this guidebook.

The following is a sampling of the things you will discover and learn to practice on your journey through these daily lessons and readings:

- God's plan of redemption is revealed repeatedly throughout the people and events of the Old Testament.
- The person, life, and ministry of Jesus were prefigured in many of the Bible's stories.
- Studying and meditating on the symbolic significance of Bible stories can enlarge and enrich your understanding and experience of Jesus and his love for you.
- Your salvation in Christ is much deeper and richer than you have previously understood.
- Jesus is a mighty Savior—a Second Adam, a New Elijah, a New Jonah, the Rebel King, and the Living Temple.
- Encountering Jesus as the Pioneer of Faith, the Victor in Death, the Fourth Man, the Lifter of the Curse—and more—

can deepen and broaden your love for him like never before.
- There are layers of meaning and symbolism in the Passion and Resurrection of Jesus that can make those events even more impactful for you, your family, friends, and church.
- Your reading and study of the Bible can come alive in new ways as you learn to read and study it all in the light of God's ongoing plan of redemption.
- And much more!

Finally, the life-changing benefit you derive from this study will depend, in large part, on your desire and determination to discover and put into practice the truths and insights you receive from this guidebook. It will have the greatest and longest-lasting impact if you read and use it at the same time your church and small group are participating in the campaign (see the next section, "How to Use *The Bible 30-Day Experience GuideBook*"). But whether you use it as part of a coordinated church campaign or focus on individual study, be assured that a great journey awaits you.

God bless you for taking this extraordinary step in your spiritual journey!

HOW TO USE
THE BIBLE 30-DAY EXPERIENCE GUIDEBOOK

The Apostle Paul, writing to first-century followers of Jesus in the city of Corinth, referred to some of the stories of God's people, saying:

> I do not want you to be ignorant of the fact, brothers and sisters, that our ancestors were all under the cloud and that they all passed through the sea. They were all baptized into Moses in the cloud and in the sea. They all ate the same spiritual food and drank the same spiritual drink; for they drank from the spiritual rock that accompanied them, and that rock was Christ. ...
> These things happened to them as examples and were written down as warnings for us, on whom the culmination of the ages has come
> —1 Corinthians 10:1–4,11

In those few paragraphs, Paul revealed that the stories of God's people from long ago had important, current application to God's people of that day. He also showed them that Jesus was present in those stories in ways that people had not recognized or understood at the time. He was the rock in the wilderness. He was the manna and the water. He was there all along because God was always accomplishing his purpose of redemption.

So it is with the stories of the epic TV miniseries, *The Bible*, which is the basis of *The Bible 30-Day Experience DVD Study* and *The Bible 30-Day Experience GuideBook*, which you hold in your hands. Through these pages, and your reading and study over the next thirty days, you will encounter the Bible in a new way. You will see it with new eyes. You will see more than ever before. You will see Jesus there. You will even see yourself, and your own story, woven through every story.

GETTING STARTED
IN *THE BIBLE 30-DAY EXPERIENCE GUIDEBOOK*

The readings in this guidebook begin on Monday (Day 1). Six daily readings are provided for each week—Monday through Saturday. There are no Sunday readings since Sundays are intended to give you a chance to rest, worship, take notes on your pastor's sermons— and even to catch up if you've fallen a bit behind in your daily readings.

To get the most from this experience, set aside a specific time each day to work on the daily lesson, reading, and follow-up materials (outlined below). This should take no more than twenty minutes, depending of course, on the rate at which you read and the degree to which you apply yourself. Take your time; don't read ahead or try to complete more than one day at a time. They are designed to build on each other and will have the maximum effect if they are done once a day, ideally, in the morning. This will allow you to process and meditate on the topic throughout the day, while also implementing the daily "Experience the Story" exercise (see below). Also, you will draw the most benefit if you try not to skip readings, which would force you to have to catch up at some point.

Each "day" in *The Bible 30-Day Experience GuideBook* contains the following content:

DAILY READING
Each day's content begins with a short reading. Most of these won't take you more than a few minutes. They are designed to get you thinking about a particular aspect of the week's topic.

FROM THE BIBLE
Carefully selected Scriptures follow the daily reading. Some are drawn from the reading, while others are intended to supplement or amplify the reading. You are encouraged to look these up in your Bible and read them in their broader context.

FROM THE HEART

After the daily reading and the Scripture selections, a prayer has been included. We encourage you not only to read this prayer but also to actually pray it—out loud even. You may want to add to it or personalize it in some way in response to your personal thoughts and emotions.

DID YOU KNOW?

This short section provides additional information, interesting details, or related facts about something mentioned in the reading.

EXPERIENCE THE STORY

Every day's content includes a small, suggested exercise—requiring further action and employing other senses—to help you apply the truth or lesson of the day's reading. Sometimes practical, sometimes symbolic, they are intended to help you go beyond simply reading about a truth, and actively experience the story as well.

GO DEEPER

These suggestions are included for participants who want to further explore a story or truth discussed in the reading.

REFLECTION TIME

The final section of each day's study material is a question or series of questions for you to think about. Some days there will also be space for you to respond in writing. Take your time with this, as this activity often produces great insight and important breakthroughs for the participant.

WEEKLY REVIEW PAGE

After the Saturday reading each week there is a one-page recap, touching upon the main theme of that week. There are several ways to use this weekly review: (1) Read it after the Saturday selection each week, to close your time of study; (2) Read it before going to your weekend worship service; (3) Look over the weekly review before your small-group meeting, to refresh your mind and prepare for a meaningful study and discussion experience with others.

SMALL-GROUP STUDY AND DISCUSSION QUESTIONS

After the Weekly Review page there are two pages of small-group study and discussion questions that should be used in your small group or Sunday school class. The small-group study and discussion questions in this book are located at the end of each week; since your small group may meet earlier in the week, you may want to turn ahead in your guidebook and review the thoughts, questions, and Scriptures found in this section before your small group or Sunday school class starts. And you will want to bring the guidebook with you to that weekly meeting so you can follow along with the progression of thoughts, Scriptures, and questions being discussed.

So, are you ready to get started? Are you ready—no matter where you are right now on your spiritual journey—to engage with the stories of the Bible in a new and invigorating way? Are you ready to have a deeper encounter with the God of the Bible than you've ever experienced before? Are you ready to see Jesus and experience his presence more powerfully than ever before? Then let's get going in *The Bible 30-Day Experience GuideBook*!

WEEK ONE THEME:

FROM DEATH TO LIFE

MAIN MESSAGE POINT:

GOD'S GREAT PLAN OF SALVATION PROVIDES A WAY OUT FOR ME—OUT OF DEATH AND INTO LIFE—NEW LIFE, ETERNAL LIFE, ABUNDANT LIFE.

THIS WEEK'S MEMORY VERSE:

"WHOEVER HEARS MY WORD AND BELIEVES HIM WHO SENT ME HAS ETERNAL LIFE AND WILL NOT BE JUDGED BUT HAS CROSSED OVER FROM DEATH TO LIFE."
—JOHN 5:24

THE HEAVENLY MAN

Perhaps there was a moment, the instant before he opened his eyes, when the first man awoke to the fact that he was alive.

Can you imagine? One moment he was inanimate and insentient; the next moment, he was alive and aware. One moment he wasn't, and then a moment later, he was.

The Bible doesn't fill in all the details, but it makes sense to imagine that Adam, the first man (whose name means, "dirt man" or "earthling") awoke in wonder on the first day of his existence. He must have opened his eyes to a dazzling array of newness and beauty.

His newly focused eyes were the first to gaze on trees ... and toucans. His ears tuned in to rustling leaves ... and thundering waterfalls. The cool evening breeze on his face, the juice of an orange on his tongue, the sweet smell of honeysuckle, all flooded his new consciousness with first-time sensations.

What must those first days have been like? Did he exhaust himself like a child at his first carnival? Did he sample all the pleasures of the garden until he could scarcely absorb more? We don't know, of course, but it is not hard to believe that the first man had plenty to keep him busy. And then, after his loving Creator provided a woman as a partner in all those pleasures, his joy and fulfillment could not have been more complete.

But at some point, it all went south.

Tempted in the Garden, those human prototypes became human tragedies. They disobeyed their loving, generous Creator. They ignored his command. They disregarded his warning. They sinned. And when sin entered the world, death came with it. The Bible says,

"Sin entered the world through one man, and death through sin, and in this way death came to all people" (Romans 5:12).

But that is hardly the end of the story.

Many generations after Adam's fall, a Second Adam came. But, oh, the difference! Adam's physical body was created, and then he became "a living being" (Genesis 2:7); the Second Adam existed from eternity, and took up residence in a human body (Colossians 2:9). The First Adam awoke to new existence fully grown, in a lush Garden; the Second Adam entered his earthly existence as a baby in a crude manger. "The first man was of the dust of the earth; the second man is of heaven" (1 Corinthians 15:47). The First Adam, tempted in a Garden, gave in to temptation; the Second Adam, tempted in a desert wilderness, conquered every temptation and remained sinless (Hebrews 4:15). The first Adam received life as a gift and chose death by sinning; the Second Adam embraced death as the way to life, not for himself but for all who believe in him.

The Second Adam is more commonly known by the name Jesus, of course. And by far the most important distinction between him and our first ancestor is this: Adam bequeathed a curse, while Jesus bestows on us a gift. Paul, the great first-century church planter, said,

> "The gift is not like the trespass. For if the many died by the trespass of the one man, how much more did God's grace and the gift that came by the grace of the one man, Jesus Christ, overflow to the many! Nor can the gift of God be compared with the result of one man's sin: The judgment followed one sin and brought condemnation, but the gift followed many trespasses and brought justification. For if, by the trespass of the one man, death reigned through that one man, how much more will those who receive God's abundant provision of grace and of the gift of righteousness reign in life through the one man, Jesus Christ!"
> —Romans 5:15–17

Jesus came to reverse the curse (John 10:10). He is the Second Adam. The "heavenly man" (1 Corinthians 15:48). And by his life, death, and resurrection, he will lead those who trust in Him from death … to life.

FROM THE BIBLE

If there is a natural body, there is also a spiritual body. So it is written: "The first man Adam became a living being"; the last Adam, a life-giving spirit. The spiritual did not come first, but the natural, and after that the spiritual. The first man was of the dust of the earth; the second man is of heaven. As was the earthly man, so are those who are of the earth; and as is the heavenly man, so also are those who are of heaven. And just as we have borne the image of the earthly man, so shall we bear the image of the heavenly man.
—*1 Corinthians 15:44–49*

Consequently, just as one trespass resulted in condemnation for all people, so also one righteous act resulted in justification and life for all people. For just as through the disobedience of the one man the many were made sinners, so also through the obedience of the one man the many will be made righteous.
—*Romans 5:18–19*

"I came to give life—life in all its fullness" (Jesus).
—*John 10:10, NCV*

FROM THE HEART

Gracious God, thank you for this thirty-day journey into your Word. Help me to see in these stories not only my life story that you have written, but also to truly and repeatedly encounter Jesus in its pages. Thank you also for sending Jesus, the Second Adam, to reverse the curse and deliver me from sin and death. Let his life control my life today and through this week. In Jesus' name, amen.

DID YOU KNOW?

A. W. Tozer wrote, "Jesus Christ did infinitely more in His death and resurrection than just undoing the damage of the fall. He came to raise us into the image of Jesus Christ, not merely to the image of the first Adam. ... Redemption in Christ, then, is not to pay back dollar-for-dollar or to straighten man out and restore him into Adamic grace. The purpose and work of redemption in Christ Jesus is to raise man as much above the level of Adam as Christ Himself is above the level of Adam. We are to gaze upon Christ, not Adam, and in so doing are being transformed by the Spirit of God into Christ's image."[1]

EXPERIENCE THE STORY: LOOK IN THE MIRROR

Every time you look in a mirror today, remind yourself that just as you bear "the image of the earthly man," you also bear "the image of the heavenly man," Jesus, as a result of his saving grace to you.

GO DEEPER

For further study, read Paul's thoughts on the contrast between Adam and Jesus in Romans 5:12–21.

REFLECTION TIME

Today is the first day of *The Bible 30-Day Experience* in this journal. Take a few minutes to jot down your hopes and expectations for these next thirty days.

- How would I like to be different thirty days from now?
- What do I want God to do for me? In me? Through me?

COME INTO THE ARK

How did God break the news to Noah? Did he appear to him in a dream or vision? Did an angel appear in Noah's kitchen? Did he hear whispers in the night?

We don't know. The Bible only tells us that Noah lived in a world that had become so wicked, God resolved to destroy it with a flood—but not Noah, or Noah's family.

God somehow told Noah of his plans. He instructed him to build a massive boat that would become the means of salvation for Noah and his wife, their three sons and their wives. And Noah obeyed, even to the point of stocking the vessel with every creature of the land and air—and food to keep them all alive.

When that was done, the rains came. And the waters rose. And the earth's surface flooded. And the wicked perished. But God saved Noah and his family.

It is a story both engrossing and frightening. But it is more than that. It actually points to another story—and even to your own story. You see, Noah's ark is considered by many to be a type of the Lord Jesus Christ. A "type" is a story or personality in Scripture that points to a future reality (there are also "anti-types," such as Adam, who is the anti-type of Jesus). There are many ways in which the ark that saved Noah and his family can be seen as a symbol of Jesus and his salvation. For example:

1. Salvation comes by grace. "Noah found grace in the eyes of the LORD" (Genesis 6:8, KJV), and the salvation provided through Jesus is likewise a salvation "by grace ... through faith" (Ephesians 2:8a, ERV). No one deserves to be saved, for "all have sinned and fall short of the glory of God, [but] all are justified freely by his grace through the redemption that came by Christ Jesus" (Romans 3:23–24).

2. Salvation comes by invitation. After Noah had managed to build the ark and assemble the animals and provisions, "the LORD said to Noah, 'Come into the ark, you and all your household'" (Genesis 7:1, NKJV). God had already shown

marvelous grace to Noah, by unfolding his great and mysterious plans to him; but the salvation God provided was still offered to Noah. It was his to accept or reject, much like the invitation extended by Jesus, who says, "Come to me, all you who are weary and burdened, and I will give you rest" (Matthew 11:28).

3. Those who are saved enter by the door. Noah was commanded to "put a door in the side of the ark" (Genesis 6:16). And, when all the creatures and Noah's entire family had gathered inside, the Bible says, "Then the LORD shut him in" (Genesis 7:16b). Similarly, Jesus identified himself as the way to the Father (John 14:6) and as the Door (John 10:9) through which all are saved.

4. All who are saved pass through the waters and are cleansed. The ark delivered all who trusted in it safely through the water, a parallel with the waters of baptism, according to the Apostle Peter. He wrote, "In the days of Noah while the ark was being built ... only a few people, eight in all, were saved through water, and this water symbolizes baptism that now saves you also—not the removal of dirt from the body but the pledge of a clear conscience toward God. It saves you by the resurrection of Jesus Christ, who has gone into heaven and is at God's right hand—with angels, authorities and powers in submission to him" (1 Peter 3:20b–22).

Those are just some of the ways the story of Noah points to your story, the story of everyone who finds salvation through faith in Jesus Christ. It is the story of every soul who has escaped death by believing what God says and trusting him to save. It is the story of every soul who has been lifted out of this world's sin and death, and brought into a new kind of life—resurrection life.

FROM THE BIBLE

Now the earth was corrupt in God's sight and was full of violence. God saw how corrupt the earth had become, for all the people on earth had corrupted their ways. So God said to Noah, "I am going to put an end to all people, for the earth is filled with violence because

of them. I am surely going to destroy both them and the earth. So make yourself an ark."
—*Genesis 6:11–14a*

By faith Noah, when warned about things not yet seen, in holy fear built an ark to save his family. By his faith he condemned the world and became heir of the righteousness that is in keeping with faith.
—*Hebrews 11:7*

Just as it was in the days of Noah, so also will it be in the days of the Son of Man. People were eating, drinking, marrying and being given in marriage up to the day Noah entered the ark. Then the flood came and destroyed them all.
—*Luke 17:26–27*

FROM THE HEART
Lord God, you saved Noah and his family, and in doing so provided a shadow of things to come. Thank you for salvation by grace. Thank you for Jesus' kind invitation. Thank you for providing a way of salvation. Thank you that I, like Noah, have by grace become an heir of the righteousness that is in keeping with faith. In Jesus' name, amen.

DID YOU KNOW?
Similarly to the Apostle Peter's first letter, which compares God's deliverance of those who were in Noah's ark with Christian baptism, early Christian theologians saw parallels between the ark and the Church (i.e., the church is like the ark in that salvation can be found only through union with Christ and his Body, the Church).

EXPERIENCE THE STORY:
PASS THROUGH THE WATERS
If you have trusted in Jesus for salvation, but have not yet submitted to baptism as a testimony and outward symbol of your death to sin and resurrection to life in Christ, contact the leaders of your church and arrange to be baptized as soon as possible.

GO DEEPER

For further study, read the entire account of the flood in Genesis 6, 7, and 8.

REFLECTION TIME

Choose one or more of the following to reflect on and then write your response in the space below :

- Jesus said, "Just as it was in the days of Noah, so also will it be in the days of the Son of Man. People were eating, drinking, marrying and being given in marriage up to the day Noah entered the ark. Then the flood came and destroyed them all" (Luke 17:26–27). How are my times like the days of Noah? How are they different?
- I may not have an ark to build, but there are certainly some tasks God wants me to accomplish before Jesus returns and time comes to an end. What are the most important tasks, and how can I better focus on them?

THE PIONEER OF FAITH

Ur was already an ancient city in the early days of Abraham's life. A fine place to call home, it possessed a towering temple, a thriving marketplace, prosperous artisans and merchants, and all the surrounding pastureland that an established tribal chief like Abraham could want.

But God spoke to him, somehow, back when his name was Abram, before it was changed to Abraham. Maybe he heard a voice in the night. Maybe God appeared to him in a dream. Maybe it was an inner conviction that grew, little by little, until Abraham could no longer ignore it. We don't know. The Bible doesn't say. It simply tells us:

The LORD … said to Abram, "Go from your country, your people and your father's household to the land I will show you. I will make you into a great nation, and I will bless you" (Genesis 12:1–2).

And Abraham went. Perhaps he balked at first. He may have argued with God. He might have asked for more details—maybe even some concessions ("Can you send me a nice offer on my house?" or "Can it wait until after the playoffs?"). But whatever his initial reaction was—however long it took him to make the final decision—he did it. He left his home, his neighbors and friends, everything he had ever known, and set out for the land of Canaan, a journey of roughly eight hundred miles from Ur.

The safe: surrendered.

The familiar: gone.

The comfortable: left behind.

But with the call came a promise, or rather a series of promises: God would make him "the father of many nations" (Genesis 17:4). His descendants would be kings (Genesis 17:6). His name would be great (Genesis 12:2). Those were all extremely important things in those days. Having many descendants was a form of security, a safety net for one's old age. A king or two in the family certainly wouldn't hurt, either—especially when tribal warfare and blood feuds could wipe out entire clans. And a "great name" was more highly valued by the wise than flocks and lands and gold or silver; those things could all be stolen or destroyed, but a great name was a lasting inheritance.

So Abraham obeyed. He believed God. He left home and set off on a long and demanding journey. And God fulfilled his promises to Abraham—every last one.

Many years later, there was Another who left his home for a far-off land. There was Another who left behind the safe, the familiar, the comfortable, for a journey of unfathomable distance.

Like Abraham, when the Father called, Jesus said, "Here I am, I have come to do your will" (Hebrews 10:9).

Like Abraham, he left his Father's household and journeyed a long way—from the very throne of heaven to a virgin's womb, "being made in human likeness" (Philippians 2:7b)—and thus becoming the pioneer of our faith (Hebrews 12:2).

Like Abraham, he obeyed. "He humbled himself, by becoming obedient to death—even death on a cross" (Philippians 2:8) to open the way to eternal life for all who would trust in him and follow him.

Abraham was the type. Jesus is the fulfillment. And, as he did for Abraham, the Father kept his promise to Jesus in raising him from the dead, exalting him to the place of highest honor (Philippians 2:9) and making him the "father" of a holy nation, a nation of kings (1 Peter 2:9), at whose great name "every knee should bow, in heaven and on earth and under the earth, and every tongue acknowledge that Jesus Christ is Lord, to the glory of God the Father" (Philippians 2:10b–11).

FROM THE BIBLE

By faith Abraham, when called to go to a place he would later receive as his inheritance, obeyed and went, even though he did not know where he was going.
—*Hebrews 11:8*

What does Scripture say? "Abraham believed God, and it was credited to him as righteousness."
—*Romans 4:3*

Understand, then, that those who have faith are children of Abraham.
—*Galatians 3:7*

In your relationships with one another, have the same mindset as Christ Jesus:

Who, being in very nature God, did not consider equality with God something to be used to his own advantage;
rather, he made himself nothing by taking the very nature of a servant, being made in human likeness.
And being found in appearance as a man, he humbled himself by becoming obedient to death—
     even death on a cross!
Therefore God exalted him to the highest place and gave him the name that is above every name,
that at the name of Jesus every knee should bow, in heaven and on earth and under the earth,
and every tongue acknowledge that Jesus Christ is Lord, to the glory of God the Father.
—*Philippians 2:5–11*

FROM THE HEART

Lord Jesus, thank you for your glorious condescension in leaving your glory in heaven and journeying to earth, to a virgin's womb, to a Bethlehem stable, for me. Thank you that such infinite distance was not too far for you, and that the crudeness of human birth and life, suffering and death were not too much for You to give because of Your great love for me. Thank you for Your remarkable sacrifice for me. Amen.

DID YOU KNOW?

Two titles repeatedly given to Abraham in Scripture are "Father of many nations" (Genesis 17:5, Romans 4:17) and "the friend of God" (2 Chronicles 20:7, Isaiah 41:8, James 2:23).

EXPERIENCE THE STORY: DOORS

Each time you step through a door today—to a room, an office, a car, etc.—give thanks for the journey Jesus took and the distance Jesus traveled for your salvation.

GO DEEPER

For further study, you will find the story of Abraham's call in Genesis 12 and God's covenant with Abraham in Genesis 15.

REFLECTION TIME

Take a few moments to reflect on the following and write your thoughts in the space below:

- What does "home" mean to me—and why?
- What would it take for me to leave home for an unknown destination?
- How do the answers to the above affect my feelings about Jesus leaving heaven for me?

THREE MEN AND A BABY

It was the hottest part of the day in the Judean hills. It's best for an old man to stay in the shade at such times and not exert oneself.

Then again, when you can go weeks and months without meeting anyone new, without seeing anyone outside your own family and flocks, it is a potential holiday when you see three human forms materialize on the horizon.

So Abraham, who had been sitting in the shade at the entrance of his tent, rose from his cushions and shuffled toward the travelers. There were three of them. He hurried in their direction, afraid they might pass by without stopping.

Like the Mideastern tribal chief he was, he bowed low as he advanced toward them. Displaying the kind of hospitality typical in desert culture, he invited them to stay. "If you would be so kind, please stay for a visit. Let me provide water to wash your dusty feet. Rest for awhile in the shade while food is prepared, before you continue your journey."

The three men agreed, so Abraham happily clapped his hands together and ducked back into his tent. He told his wife, Sarah, to get started making bread, and personally selected a calf from his herd for a servant to butcher and roast. Then he returned to the travelers with goat's milk and curds to begin the feast.

One of the men asked for his wife, calling her by name. Abraham said she was in the tent. The traveler said, "I will surely return to you about this time next year, and Sarah your wife will have a son" (Genesis 18:10a).

Sarah, who had been eavesdropping, laughed at the man's words. The traveler heard her laugh, and asked, "Is anything too hard for the Lord?" He repeated his prediction.

When the travelers finished the feast Abraham had provided, two resumed their journey—for Sodom. But the one who foretold a child for Sarah stayed, and revealed to Abraham the Lord's plans to destroy Sodom and Gomorrah because of their great wickedness.

The Bible account of that incident, in Genesis 18, repeatedly uses Yahweh, the name of God, to refer to the Traveler who spoke to Abraham. And many scholars see in those scenes a Christophany, an Old Testament appearance of Jesus Christ.

In any case, the Traveler who promised a child to Sarah and entertained Abraham's petitions for the cities of Sodom and Gomorrah foreshadows the coming of Jesus to earth as the Messenger of God. Like Abraham's visitor, Jesus spoke gracious promises to his loved ones; some have listed more than two hundred promises Jesus made! Also like Abraham's visitor, Jesus graciously hears and grants our petitions and intercessions; he says, "You may ask me for anything in my name, and I will do it" (John 14:14).

And there is at least one more way in which Abraham's chief visitor parallels Jesus. If you look closely at Genesis 18, in which Abraham intercedes for Sodom and Gomorrah, you will see something important. Abraham asks the Lord if he would spare the cities if fifty righteous people were found in them (Genesis 18:24), and the Lord says he would do so. Next, Abraham asks the Lord if he would spare Sodom and Gomorrah for the sake of forty-five righteous people (Genesis 18:28), and the Lord says he would do so. Abraham presses his case, reducing the number to forty (Genesis 18:29), then thirty (Genesis 18:30), twenty (Genesis 18:31), and even ten (Genesis 18:32). And the Lord agrees to withhold judgment for the sake of ten righteous people in the city. But apparently, Abraham stops asking. The chapter concludes with the words, "When the LORD had finished speaking with Abraham, he left, and Abraham returned home" (Genesis 18:33).

Here's the point: Abraham apparently stopped asking before the Lord stopped answering! Abraham stopped at the number ten. What if he had kept interceding for five? Or even one? Would those cities have been spared?

We don't know. But we do know this. Like Abraham's visitor,

Jesus connects his continued answers to our continued asking, saying, "Keep on asking, and you will receive what you ask for" (Matthew 7:7, NLT). May we never stop asking until he answers. And may we never stop until he has finished giving us what we ask.

FROM THE BIBLE

The LORD appeared to Abraham near the great trees of Mamre while he was sitting at the entrance to his tent in the heat of the day.
—*Genesis 18:1*

The men turned away and went toward Sodom, but Abraham remained standing before the LORD.
—*Genesis 18:22*

Do not forget to show hospitality to strangers, for by so doing some people have shown hospitality to angels without knowing it.
—*Hebrews 13:2*

"Keep on asking, and you will receive what you ask for. Keep on seeking, and you will find. Keep on knocking, and the door will be opened to you."
—*Matthew 7:7, NLT*

FROM THE HEART

Lord Jesus, thank you for your words of promise. Thank you for your promise of answered prayer. Teach me to keep on asking, keep on seeking, keep on knocking, until I fully apprehend answers to my prayers. Help me to intercede for others, as Abraham did for Sodom, but never to stop asking before you are finished giving, in Jesus' name, amen.

DID YOU KNOW?

Some scholars see Jesus' words in John 8:56 ("Your father Abraham rejoiced at the thought of seeing my day; he saw it and was glad") as a reference to Abraham meeting Jesus and conversing with him at the above incident in Genesis 18.

EXPERIENCE THE STORY: REIGNITE A REQUEST

Is there a need you have stopped bringing to the Lord in prayer? Is there someone for whom you once interceded regularly but then gave up at some point? If so, reignite that request (especially if it is intercession for someone who has not yet moved from death to new life in Christ). Start asking again, and "keep asking" until the Lord grants your request—no matter how long that takes.

GO DEEPER

For further study, read the full account of Abraham's three visitors at Mamre and the subsequent events in Genesis 18–19.

REFLECTION TIME

Jesus said to "Keep on asking. … Keep on seeking, and, … Keep on knocking" (Matthew 7:7, NLT). Take some time to list:
- one thing I will keep asking
- one thing I will keep seeking
- one door I will keep knocking on until it opens

IN THE NICK OF TIME

It was a valid question. In fact, it may have been the most valid question any child ever asked.

It wasn't, "Why?" It wasn't, "Where do babies come from?" It wasn't, "Are we there yet?" (though it so happens that last one would have applied).

The question was, "Where is the lamb?"

Isaac asked it after he and his father, Abraham, had been traveling for a couple days, and finally approached their destination: the blunt height of Mount Moriah, a stone outcropping in the Judean hills, surrounded by landscape brown and gray, rough and rocky.

Isaac knew they were going there to worship. Which meant they would make a sacrifice. But something was missing. Something crucial—indispensible, in fact.

They had carted a bundle of wood all the way from home, lashed now to Isaac's back. Abraham carried the ceremonial knife for the sacrifice in his belt; Isaac had seen the polished handle glimmer in the sun. Abraham also held the pot with the coals from their breakfast fire, which would be used to ignite their offering. But something was still missing.

So Isaac asked. "Father," he said. "I see we have the fire and wood, but where is the lamb for the burnt offering?"

A reasonable question, especially since the harsh landscape offered little hope of happening upon such an animal. Were there settlements somewhere in these hills where a lamb could be bought?

Abraham answered, "God will provide the lamb."

That was it. No elaboration. No detail. Just, "God will provide the lamb."

Abraham's answer may be a hint of his faith. Or he may have been stalling for time, putting off the moment when he would have to reveal the awful truth to Isaac. That he would be bound hand and foot, that he would be laid on the altar, that his throat would be cut. That he was the sacrifice.

But Isaac soon got the point—almost literally, in fact. It was only after Abraham had bound his son, laid him on the altar, and raised the knife to end the boy's life that God provided the lamb. In an instant, arrested by the voice of an angel and the appearance of a ram in a nearby bush, Isaac was delivered from death and given new life.

Finally.

Just in time.

Not a moment too soon.

Many years later, a similar scenario took place. The Bible says, "When the set time had fully come, God sent his Son" (Galatians 4:4). In the nick of time, like the ram God sent to Abraham, Jesus appeared. Like the ram, his coming was announced by an angel. Like the ram, tangled in a thicket, Jesus wore a crown of thorns. And, like the ram, he died as a sacrifice.

The Bible says, "Abraham called that place The LORD Will Provide. And to this day it is said, 'On the mountain of the LORD it will be provided'" (Genesis 22:14). Author, theologian, and pastor R. C. Sproul points out, "It was on Mount Moriah, later named Mount Calvary, just outside of Jerusalem, where two thousand years after Abraham's experience, our Savior on the night before His death went into the Garden of Gethsemane. With sweat drops of blood He pleaded with the Father to allow the cup to pass from Him. 'Nevertheless,' Jesus said, 'Not what I will, but what You will' (Mark 14:36). In that moment of the grand passion of Christ, the Father said no. The Father would not spare His Son."[2]

As the ram in the thicket took Isaac's place, Jesus took your place. You may have long been ignorant of your danger, as Isaac was of his. But perhaps there came a moment when the truth dawned on you— when your eyes were opened to the urgency of your situation. You became aware of your need to be rescued, and how hopeless your situation would be if God had not provided a substitute … in the nick of time.

But he did. Your lamb among thorns, however, was God's own son. Your substitution was the Lamb of God, who takes away the sin of the world. "[God] did not spare his own Son, but gave him up for us all" (Romans 8:32a), so we can escape death and enjoy life—everlasting, and abundant.

FROM THE BIBLE

Then God said, "Take your son, your only son, whom you love—Isaac—and go to the region of Moriah. Sacrifice him there as a burnt offering on a mountain I will show you."
—Genesis 22:1

Abraham looked up and there in a thicket he saw a ram caught by its horns. He went over and took the ram and sacrificed it as a burnt offering instead of his son. So Abraham called that place The LORD Will Provide. And to this day it is said, "On the mountain of the LORD it will be provided."
—Genesis 22:13–14

By faith Abraham, when God tested him, offered Isaac as a sacrifice. He who had embraced the promises was about to sacrifice his one and only son, even though God had said to him, "It is through Isaac that your offspring will be reckoned." Abraham reasoned that God could even raise the dead, and so in a manner of speaking he did receive Isaac back from death.
—Hebrews 11:17–19

Your old life is dead. Your new life, which is your real life—even though invisible to spectators—is with Christ in God. He is your life.
—Colossians 3:3–4a (MSG)

FROM THE HEART

Father God, thank you for sending Jesus "in the fullness of time" to be my substitute, a sacrifice for my sins, and the means by which I pass from death to life. Help me to live a life worthy of such a great salvation. Let my daily life reflect the deliverance that is mine through the suffering of Jesus, in whose name I ask, amen.

DID YOU KNOW?

The original Hebrew of Genesis 22:14 allows for two possible translations—"On the mountain of the LORD it will be provided" and "On the mountain the LORD will appear"—both of which were fulfilled in Jesus' sacrificial death on Calvary.

EXPERIENCE THE STORY: GET THE POINT

If you see or use a knife today—for cooking, perhaps—take a moment to reflect on the relief Isaac must have felt when his father's raised knife was halted by the voice of an angel and the appearance of the ram in the thicket. Realize that your passage from death to life via the appearance and sacrifice of Jesus is no less real than what Isaac must have felt that day on Mount Moriah.

GO DEEPER

For further study, read the full account of the binding of Isaac in Genesis 22.

REFLECTION TIME

Apostle Paul, writing to the Colossians, referred to Jesus, saying, "He is your life." List three or more ways that truth is real in your experience:

_____

_____

_____

_____

_____

_____

_____

_____

_____

CHRIST, OUR PASSOVER LAMB

God could have done it any way he chose.

It is easy to forget that. We look back on the stories of the Bible, and because they are familiar, we forget that events didn't have to unfold as they did.

A perfect example is the Exodus, and the dramatic series of events that preceded the deliverance of the Hebrew people from slavery in Egypt. God is all-powerful; he could have rescued his people from slavery in any number of ways. He could have dictated terms to Pharaoh and moved his lips to decree the people's release. He could have turned all the Egyptians into statues until the people of God were safely across the Red Sea. He could have simply levitated the entire population of Goshen, floated them through the air, and deposited them safely on the opposite shores of the Red Sea, out of the reach of the Egyptians. But he didn't.

Instead, God sent Moses, who announced a series of plagues that exerted God's absolute control over humans, animals, nature—and even the false gods of Egypt. But he saved his most significant, symbolic effort for last.

God sent one last plague: the death of every firstborn child in Egypt. It would visit every household. No one would escape. Though the Hebrews had been exempted from previous plagues, there would be no exception made this time, unless they submitted to God's plan.

God told them, "Each man is to take a lamb for his family, one for each household" (Exodus 12:3b). It had to be a year-old male lamb, without defect. It was to be sacrificed, and the blood smeared at the top and on each side of the doorframe at the entrance to their homes.

The blood of a lamb. A young lamb. A male. A spotless lamb. Put to death. And they were instructed to stain the doorways of their homes in three places: top, left-hand side, right-hand side. And God promised that every household who trusted him enough to submit to those procedures would be saved from the angel of death. He assured them that the angel of death would "pass over" every house that was thus protected.

Why? Remember, God could have accomplished the deliverance of his people any way he wanted. He could have given the angel of death the address of every Hebrew household in the land. But the means he chose involved a sacrificial, spotless lamb whose blood stained the top and sides of every door. Again, why?

It is not hard at all to understand when we recall that many years later the spotless Lamb of God would be announced by John the Baptist by the river Jordan (John 1:29). And that Jesus would foreshadow his own death on the night of his arrest with the Passover meal prescribed by God through Moses—by breaking bread and explaining, "This is my body given for you," and lifting the symbolic cup of salvation and saying, "This cup is the new covenant in my blood, which is poured out for you" (Luke 22:19–20). And that he would be sacrificed on a cruel Roman cross stained by the blood from his pierced hands and thorn-crowned head, in the pattern made on the doorways by the Hebrew slaves in Egypt. And that with his very last utterance on the cross he would speak the words used by a priest when the last lamb of Passover was killed, the Hebrew word, kalah: "It is finished!" (John 19:30).

As Apostle Paul would write to the church at Corinth, "Christ, our Passover Lamb, has been sacrificed" (1 Corinthians 5:7). His death delivers you from death, if you have done as Jesus said: "Whoever hears my word and believes him who sent me has eternal life and will not be judged but has crossed over from death to life" (John 5:24).

FROM THE BIBLE

On that same night I will pass through Egypt and strike down every firstborn of both people and animals, and I will bring judgment on all the gods of Egypt. I am the LORD. The blood will be a sign for you on the houses where you are, and when I see the blood, I will pass over you. No destructive plague will touch you when I strike Egypt.
—*Exodus 12:12–13*

The next day John saw Jesus coming toward him and said, "Look, the Lamb of God, who takes away the sin of the world!"
—*John 1:29*

When he had received the drink, Jesus said, "It is finished." With that, he bowed his head and gave up his spirit.
—*John 19:30*

Christ, our Passover lamb, has been sacrificed.
—*1 Corinthians 5:7*

FROM THE HEART

Lord God, how carefully you planned my salvation! How beautifully you wrote the story of my deliverance on every page of your Word! Thank you for the wonders of your amazing plan, and for unfolding it as you did through the rescue of your people from slavery in Egypt and the sacrificial love of Jesus on Calvary. Help me to live my daily life in the complete and constant awareness of this great salvation. In Jesus' name, amen.

DID YOU KNOW?

Commentator Matthew Henry suggests some of the many layers of meaning in the action of applying the blood of the lamb to the doorposts: "It was to be sprinkled on the door-posts, denoting the open profession we are to make of faith in Christ. It was not to be sprinkled upon the threshold; which cautions us to take heed of trampling under foot the blood of the covenant. It is precious blood, and must be precious to us. The blood, thus sprinkled, was a means of preserving the Israelites from the destroying angel, who had nothing to do where the blood was."[3]

EXPERIENCE THE STORY: DRAW A CROSS

When the Hebrew slaves in Egypt smeared the blood of the lamb on the lintels of their homes, they were foreshadowing the shape of Jesus' cross. Chances are, today you will sign or write something on a piece of paper. When you do, draw a cross, too, to remind yourself that "Christ, your Passover lamb, has been sacrificed."

GO DEEPER

For further study, read the full account of the Passover in Exodus 12, and its prescribed observance in Israel in Deuteronomy 16:1–8.

REFLECTION TIME

Tomorrow is the second Sunday in this thirty-day experience. Take a few moments to list some ways you can prepare to make tomorrow's worship as meaningful as possible.

_____

_____

_____

_____

_____

_____

_____

_____

_____

_____

If you've ever read through the Bible chronologically, you may have seen something that many people miss: It is not a collection of disparate pieces of a puzzle, but one unified story of God and his ways with his people. From the first pages to the last, the Bible tells a story, and though it employs many different forms to do so, one thing binds all the forms together—God's love for us, and his redemptive plans from beginning to end.

In the Garden of Eden, though they had every comfort and blessing a human being could wish for, our first parents listened to the tempter and disobeyed God's command, bringing sorrow—and death—onto themselves and all their descendants. So God sent a Second Adam, born of woman, to crush the head of the serpent and overcome death with new life.

God spoke to a man named Noah, whose ark became the means by which Noah's whole family was saved from a devastating flood and given a new beginning—foreshadowing One who would come and bring salvation by grace, through faith.

God called Abraham to leave his home for a far-off place, thus becoming the father of many nations, prefiguring a time in the future when Jesus would leave his home in heaven and travel an infinite distance to a virgin's womb in order to become the Savior of the world.

Over and over again, God made his intention clear and foreshadowed the coming of Jesus in multiple ways—in a lamb in a thicket, and blood on a lintel, for example—"in keeping with the revelation of the mystery hidden for long ages past" (Romans 16:25). Over and over again, God made clear his power and intention of saving his people from death—in the flood, in the destruction of Sodom and Gomorrah, on Mount Moriah, and through the Red Sea—and leading them into new and abundant life.

As you complete Week One of this experience, take a few moments to reflect on the genius and grace of God, whose power to lead us from death to life flows through so many of the Bible's stories. And take some time before beginning Week Two to reflect on the experience of this past week. Make sure you spend time in worship with others as Week Two kicks off.

WEEK ONE: SMALL-GROUP STUDY AND DISCUSSION QUESTIONS

Below is a complete list of small-group study and discussion questions for small groups that use this guidebook in conjunction with *The Bible 30-Day Experience DVD Study.* In order to stay within the time limits of your small-group meeting, your small-group leader will choose what questions he or she wants your group to focus on. You will want to bring this guidebook with you to your small group or class.

1. Open in prayer.

2. Go around the room asking everyone to briefly answer this question: "What is the farthest journey you've ever taken?"

3. Watch video: "The Binding of Isaac."

4. Question: "As you watch that video, do you find yourself identifying with anyone? If so, whom? And why?"

5. Read Genesis 22:1–19.

6. Question: "Why do you think God was so specific in verse 2 when he told Abraham, "Take your son, your only son, whom you love—Isaac …?"

7. Question: "The Bible uses only thirty words in verses 9 and 10 to describe what must have been an emotional, even tragic scene: 'He bound his son Isaac and laid him on the altar, on top of the wood. Then he reached out his hand and took the knife to slay his son.' What unrecorded words/emotions/actions do you imagine taking place in those moments?"

8. Question: "In verse 12, God said to Abraham, 'Now I know that you fear God, because you have not withheld from me your son, your only son.' Doesn't God know everything? Why do you think God took as long as he did and let Abraham go as far as he did, if God already knew what was going to happen?"

9. Question: "Notice that God refers repeatedly to Isaac as 'your son, your only son' (vv. 2, 12, 16). Why do you think he repeated that phrase?"

10. Question: "Look over verses 10–13 again. What do you think Isaac would have been feeling as the ram was slaughtered and sacrificed? As he and his father traveled back?"

11. Read Hebrews 11:17–19.

12. Question: "What light—if any—do those verses shed on the reading from Genesis 22?

13. Question: "Isaac lived many years (he lived to the age of 180!) after he nearly died on Mount Moriah. How do you think his experience on Mount Moriah might have affected him in the remaining years of his life?"

14. Question: "Does this story reflect your experience in any way? If so, how?"

15. Question: "What are some ways this story should or can reflect your experience in the future?"

16. Any other questions or comments?

17. Close in prayer.

WEEK TWO THEME:

FROM SLAVERY TO FREEDOM

MAIN MESSAGE POINT:

THE "GREAT SALVATION" GOD PROVIDES INCLUDES DELIVERANCE FROM BONDAGE AND SLAVERY, INTO A LIFE OF FREEDOM AND BLESSING.

THIS WEEK'S MEMORY VERSE:

"YOU WILL KNOW THE TRUTH, AND THE TRUTH WILL SET YOU FREE." —JOHN 8:32

THE RED ROPE

If middle school taught us anything, it taught us this: Labels can be limiting. Cutting. Confining. Enslaving, even.

Human beings are extremely complex organisms, physically, emotionally, mentally, and spiritually. It is impossible to categorize someone with a single phrase or word. Yet we do it all the time. And when that happens, it can be difficult to shed that label. It can be very difficult to overcome a reputation, once we have it. Even in our own minds and hearts.

We know that Rahab, the woman who appears in the Bible's story of the Israelite conquest of Jericho, was many things. She was a daughter. She was a sister. She was a citizen and a businesswoman. But the description that was repeatedly—perhaps unfailingly—applied to her was this: prostitute (Joshua 2:1; 6:17, 22, 25). The Bible introduces her in that way, and continues to refer to her in that way, even when commending her faith (Hebrews 11:31). As if it is important to the story, which it is.

We know nothing about how Rahab became a prostitute, or why. We don't know much of anything, other than the bare facts of her occupation. We don't know how long she had been living and plying her trade in Jericho. But the events of Joshua 2 strongly suggest that she was ready—possibly had been ready for some time—to escape her past and her reputation. When two enemy spies came under her roof, she hid them. She diverted the authorities in their search for the spies. She negotiated with the spies for her and her family's rescue from the doomed city. And she aided the spies' escape from danger:

So she let them down by a rope through the window, for the house she lived in was part of the city wall. She said to them, "Go to the hills so the pursuers will not find you. Hide yourselves there three days until they return, and then go on your way."

Now the men had said to her, "This oath you made us swear will not be binding on us unless, when we enter the land, you have tied this scarlet cord in the window through which you let us down, and unless you have brought your father and mother, your brothers and all your family into your house" (Joshua 2:15–18).

So "she tied the scarlet cord in the window," the Bible says (Joshua 2:21b). She believed their words. She attached all her hopes for the future to a blood-red sign hanging outside the city. Somehow, though the walls of Jericho fell, its army was routed, and its inhabitants were all killed, Rahab found freedom.

A scarlet rope. We are not told where the rope came from. Did the spies bring it into the city with them? Did Rahab use it to tie up laundry bundles? Had it been a fixture of the household for years? We don't know. But we are told that it was scarlet. Why are we given that detail and not others?

Perhaps it is because it was meant to foreshadow something else. Perhaps that red rope Rahab hung outside the city wall, by which her old life was utterly demolished, and a new life was given to her, is a hint of something else. Perhaps the means by which Rahab was transported from slavery to freedom, from a prostitute in Jericho to a free citizen of a holy nation, prefigures something. Something blood-red. Something—or Someone—hung outside the city walls.

It is not so hard to imagine. Especially when one has begun to see the care and attention with which God wove his redemptive plan through other events and other situations. The writer of Hebrews says, "Jesus ... suffered outside the city gate to make the people holy through his own blood" (Hebrews 13:12). As that scarlet rope brought freedom to Rahab, the blood of Jesus frees you—from the past, from guilt, shame, sin, punishment, and condemnation. From all that would drag you down and bind you in ways that are contrary to God's holy will for you.

A sign fulfilled one day outside the walls of Jerusalem. A limp figure, red with blood—the means by which your old life was utterly demolished and a new life began. The means by which your slavery ended, and you were transformed into a free citizen of a holy nation.

FROM THE BIBLE

But Joshua spared Rahab the prostitute, with her family and all who belonged to her, because she hid the men Joshua had sent as spies to Jericho—and she lives among the Israelites to this day.
—*Joshua 6:25*

By faith the prostitute Rahab, because she welcomed the spies, was not killed with those who were disobedient.
—*Hebrews 11:31*

Therefore, there is now no condemnation for those who are in Christ Jesus, because through Christ Jesus the law of the Spirit who gives life has set you free from the law of sin and death.
—*Romans 8:1*

When the time arrived that was set by God the Father, God sent his Son, born among us of a woman, born under the conditions of the law so that he might redeem those of us who have been kidnapped by the law. Thus we have been set free to experience our rightful heritage.
—*Galatians 4:4 (MSG)*

FROM THE HEART

Almighty God, thank you for setting me free from my past. Thank you for freeing me from the guilt and shame and punishment my sins deserve, apart from the salvation that is mine in Christ. Thank you that I am no longer subject to judgment and condemnation, but am free to live, breathe, trust, serve, and rejoice through faith in the One who suffered outside the city walls to make me holy through his own blood (Hebrews 13:12). In Jesus' name, amen.

DID YOU KNOW?

The Italian poet Dante places Rahab in a place of honor in his vision of "the third heaven":

"You want to know who is in this light
Which is sparkling in this manner close by me,
As a ray of sun does in clear water.

Now know that the person inside it, who is tranquil,
Is Rahab, and when she came to join to our order,
Her presence sealed it as of the highest kind;
By this heaven, in which the cone of shadow
Which your world makes has its tip, she was taken up
Before any other in the triumph of Christ.
It was indeed appropriate to leave her
In some heaven as a palm of the great victory
Which was achieved by one palm and the other,
Because she favored the first glory
Of Joshua in the Holy Land. ..."[4]

EXPERIENCE THE STORY: WEAR SOMETHING RED

Wear (or carry with you) something red today to symbolize your salvation in Jesus Christ and to remind you of his blood, which frees you from slavery to sin, guilt, shame, punishment, and condemnation.

GO DEEPER

To dig deeper into Rahab's story, read Joshua, chapters 2 and 6.

REFLECTION TIME

The Bible says, "If the Son sets you free, you will be free indeed" (John 8:36). Answer below:

- Am I holding on to old habits of the flesh or old ways of thinking since experiencing new life in Christ?
- In what areas do I need to more fully experience the true and total freedom in Christ?

THE COMMANDER OF THE LORD'S ARMIES

All was ready. God's people camped at Gilgal, a vast multitude of men, women, and children. They had successfully surveyed their first conquest—the fortified city of Jericho. That city's leaders and residents had all heard the fearful reports of God's miraculous actions on behalf of the Israelite horde.

Now Joshua, the successor of Moses, crept close to Jericho to gather any last-minute intelligence he could. After all, the famous city had withstood countless assaults. Joshua's army had no experience in warfare, let alone siege tactics. They had ample manpower—and swords, spears, bows, and arrows—but were utterly unprepared for a situation that seemed to call for more sophisticated weaponry: battering rams, catapults, siege towers, and the like. God had led them this far, and he had clearly promised this land to his people, but Jericho was the first of many cities that stood in their way.

The seemingly insurmountable odds made the night seem darker to Joshua. His survey of the walls had only made them seem taller than before. The solitude only made him feel more alone. He sighed deeply, shook his head, and when he looked up, he saw someone standing in front of him, a drawn sword in his hand.

Joshua leaped to his feet and drew his own sword. He approached warily. He kept his voice low, aware of the watchmen on the walls of the city not far off. "Are you for us? Or for our enemies?"

"Neither," the soldier replied. "I come as commander of the army of the Lord."

Joshua did not wait for more. He did not need confirmation. He dropped his sword and fell to his knees. He pressed his face to the ground and spoke into the dirt. "What does my Lord wish to say to his servant?"

"Take off your sandals, for the place where you are standing is holy," the soldier said. He proceeded to tell Joshua that Jericho had already been defeated; Joshua and Israel simply had to follow the Lord's specific instructions to complete the victory. The Lord's instructions didn't require battering rams or siege towers, but marching, trumpet-blowing, shouting, and faith. And so it happened. Joshua and the people obeyed, Jericho's walls fell, and God's people won a great victory.

You've probably heard the story. You may have sung about those walls of Jericho. But what about the soldier with the drawn sword, the captain of the Lord's army? What was that about?

There are clues: The warrior said the spot where he stood was holy ground, like the place where Moses saw the burning bush. Joshua bowed before him, and was not discouraged or corrected from offering such worship. And one more thing (though there are others): the soldier said, "I come as commander of the army of the Lord." Interesting phrasing. "I come in this way." As though he could have appeared in other ways.

In other words, the "commander of the army of the Lord" who appeared to Joshua before the battle of Jericho was very likely the pre-incarnate Lord Jesus Christ. He appeared to encourage and instruct his servant, Joshua. And to reveal to him the path to victory, the means by which God's people would conquer the first obstacle to possessing God's promises.

The last chapters of the Bible record this scene:

> I saw heaven standing open and there before me was a white horse, whose rider is called Faithful and True. With justice he judges and wages war. ... The armies of heaven were following him, riding on white horses and dressed in fine linen, white and clean (Revelation 19:11, 14).

Jesus, the commander of the Lord's armies, not only appeared to Joshua before the battle of Jericho, he came to earth to lead you to victory. To show you the means by which you can become more than a conqueror (Romans 8:37) and possess all the promises of God (1 Corinthians 1:20) by trusting in him for salvation and, in faith, following his instructions.

FROM THE BIBLE

Now when Joshua was near Jericho, he looked up and saw a man standing in front of him with a drawn sword in his hand. Joshua went up to him and asked, "Are you for us or for our enemies?"

"Neither," he replied, "but as commander of the army of the LORD I have now come." Then Joshua fell facedown to the ground in reverence, and asked him, "What message does my Lord have for his servant?"

The commander of the LORD's army replied, "Take off your sandals, for the place where you are standing is holy." And Joshua did so.
—*Joshua 5:13–15*

Now the gates of Jericho were securely barred because of the Israelites. No one went out and no one came in.

Then the LORD said to Joshua, "See, I have delivered Jericho into your hands, along with its king and its fighting men. March around the city once with all the armed men. Do this for six days. Have seven priests carry trumpets of rams' horns in front of the ark. On the seventh day, march around the city seven times, with the priests blowing the trumpets. When you hear them sound a long blast on the trumpets, have the whole army give a loud shout; then the wall of the city will collapse and the army will go up, everyone straight in."
—*Joshua 6:1–5*

For no matter how many promises God has made, they are "Yes" in Christ. And so through him the "Amen" is spoken by us to the glory of God.
—*2 Corinthians 1:20*

FROM THE HEART

Lord Jesus, Mighty Savior, thank you for this vision of you as commander of heaven's armies. I submit to you. I bow before you, as Joshua did. I await your words. Thank You for Your grace to follow you as obediently and fully as did Joshua, and to gain all the Father has promised. In Jesus' name, amen.

DID YOU KNOW?

Martin Luther, in his hymn, "A Mighty Fortress," employed the title "Lord Sabaoth," a transliteration of a Hebrew term referring to the Lord of Hosts, or "commander of the army of the Lord," to refer to Jesus:

> Did we in our own strength confide
> Our striving would be losing;
> Were not the right man on our side,
> The man of God's own choosing.
> Doth ask who that may be;
> Christ Jesus it is He.
> Lord Sabaoth, His name.
> From age to age the same.
> And He must win the battle.

EXPERIENCE THE STORY: SUBMIT TO THE SWORD

Remember that Joshua saw the commander of the Lord's armies with a drawn sword in his hand? Remember also that the Bible says that "the word of God is … sharper than any double-edged sword" (Hebrews 4:12)? Take a few moments to imagine Jesus before you, with a sword (symbolic of his Word). He is the One who has defeated the Enemy in order for you to gain all that God has promised to you.

GO DEEPER

For further study, compare Joshua 5:13–15 with Exodus 3:1–10.

REFLECTION TIME

In response to the paragraph above, on a separate sheet of paper write out a prayer of thanksgiving to Jesus for vanquishing the Enemy of Your soul by His work on the cross. Affirm His deliverance in your life.

THE VICTOR IN DEATH

His life's story is one of the strangest in the Bible.

His name was Samson. His feats were legendary, but his flaws were fatal. He had a weakness for women. He had an apparent inability to postpone gratification. He seemed to have virtually no self-control. He alternately fought the enemies of God's people ... and flirted with them. And those may have been his best qualities!

Throughout his tumultuous life, he incited the hatred of the Philistines, who looked for every opportunity to kill him. But time after time, Samson got the better of them. And he didn't just defeat them—he repeatedly humiliated them.

Until he fell in love with a woman named Delilah. She may have sincerely cared for Samson, but the Philistines offered her a small fortune to discover—and reveal to them—the secret of the fabled warrior's strength. Though at first he toyed with her, she eventually got the answer she sought. One night, when they were alone together, Samson revealed that his strength came from his vows to God, which meant that his hair had never been cut. So that night, while Samson slept, she cut his hair and then summoned his enemies.

The Philistines captured Samson. They gouged out his eyes. They shackled him with bronze manacles. They carted him off to Gaza, the scene of one of his triumphs. They enslaved him, forcing him to grind grain in the prison. They forced him to perform for their entertainment.

But in his humiliation, his hair began to grow again. And one day he was called out to entertain them in the temple of Dagon, a Philistine deity:

When they stood him among the pillars, Samson said to the servant who held his hand, "Put me where I can feel the pillars that support the temple, so that I may lean against them." Now the temple was crowded with men and women; all the rulers of the Philistines were there, and on the roof were about three thousand men and women watching Samson perform. Then Samson prayed to the LORD, "Sovereign LORD, remember me. Please, God, strengthen me just once more, and let me with one blow get revenge on the Philistines for my two eyes" (Judges 16:25b–28).

Apparently, it wasn't just Samson's hair that grew back. Enslavement and imprisonment may have also produced repentance in him, and revived his faith, as revealed in his prayer. And then:

Samson reached toward the two central pillars on which the temple stood. Bracing himself against them, his right hand on the one and his left hand on the other, Samson said, "Let me die with the Philistines!" Then he pushed with all his might, and down came the temple on the rulers and all the people in it. Thus he killed many more when he died than while he lived (Judges 16:29–30).

Take a moment to picture it. Samson stood between two stone pillars, with a hand on each. He pushed slowly outward until the stone began to creak and crack—until the pillars started to buckle. Until he stood upright, each arm extended straight out to the side. In the form of a cross. At that moment, with a final petition, he triumphed. In his death he won his greatest victory. This most flawed of God's servants, in his very last act on earth, spread his arms in the shape of a cross, breathed a final prayer, and won a startling, unexpected victory ... by dying.

Samson's story is the last place you would expect to see a reflection of Jesus. And yet ...

In the last days of Jesus' earthly life, he too spread his arms in the shape of a cross. With a loud shout, he breathed a final prayer (Luke 23:46). Against all odds, he won a startling, unexpected victory. And he did it by dying. He "disarmed the powers and authorities [and] made a public spectacle of them, triumphing over them by the cross" (Colossians 2:15).

But Jesus accomplished far more than Samson. When Samson won his last victory, his people may have cheered, but they continued to be oppressed by the Philistines. When Jesus gave up his life and ascended on high, "he made captivity itself a captive; he gave gifts to his people" (Ephesians 4:8, NRSV). He secured your freedom and every spiritual blessing (Ephesians 1:3).

FROM THE BIBLE

The angel of the LORD appeared to [Manoah's wife] and said, "You are barren and childless, but you are going to become pregnant and give birth to a son. Now see to it that you drink no wine or other fermented drink and that you do not eat anything unclean. You will become pregnant and have a son whose head is never to be touched by a razor because the boy is to be a Nazirite, dedicated to God from the womb. He will take the lead in delivering Israel from the hands of the Philistines."
—*Judges 13:3–5*

Jesus called out with a loud voice, "Father, into your hands I commit my spirit." When he had said this, he breathed his last.
—*Luke 23:46*

FROM THE HEART

Heavenly Father, thank you that, when I was dead in my sins and in the uncircumcision of my flesh, you made me alive with Christ. You forgave all my sins, having canceled the charge of my legal indebtedness, which stood against me and condemned me; you took it away, nailing it to the cross. And not only that, but, having disarmed the powers and authorities, you made a public spectacle of them— triumphing over them by the cross! Help me to live constantly in the awareness of your great triumph and of my great freedom. In Jesus' name, amen.

DID YOU KNOW?

Researchers from Tel Aviv University recently uncovered a small stone seal depicting a human figure next to a lion at the archaeological site of Beth Shemesh, near Samson's birthplace (Samson's name is a derivative of the Hebrew shemesh, which means "sun"). The seal, dated to the twelfth century BC, may be an ancient reference to the story of Samson, who is described in Judges 14 as tearing a lion apart with his bare hands.[5]

EXPERIENCE THE STORY:
YOUR ENEMY IS CRUSHED

Sometime today, pick up a pebble or stone from the ground and carry it with you (in a pocket or purse) as a symbol of the stones that crushed Samson's enemies—and the utter victory of Jesus over your Enemy.

GO DEEPER

To dig deeper into Samson's story, read Judges, chapters 13 through 16.

REFLECTION TIME

The Bible says that Jesus "disarmed the powers and authorities [and even] made a public spectacle of them, triumphing over them by the cross." (Colossians 2:15)

- What "powers and authorities" in or over my life has Jesus disarmed (for example, "the power to shame," or "the power of fear," etc.)?
- How can I live in the awareness of Jesus' triumph over all powers and authorities?

THE LORD'S ANOINTED

The prophet Samuel's heart was heavy.

It had been heavy for some time. He had harbored such high hopes for Saul, whom he had anointed as the first king of Israel. But that was long ago. Decades. And so much had changed. The king's heart had turned away from God. Repeatedly. Stubbornly.

That was when the Lord spoke. "Quit sulking over Saul," he told the prophet. "I have rejected him as king over Israel. Fill your horn with oil and get moving."

"Where, Lord?" Samuel asked.

"Go to Jesse of Bethlehem. You will anoint one of his sons as king."

Samuel obeyed, though he knew if he anointed someone new and King Saul got wind of it, the king would surely execute Samuel, prophet or not. But he went to Bethlehem nonetheless. He arranged with the town elders to sacrifice a heifer to the Lord, without a word of his plans.

When he saw Eliab, the oldest of Jesse's sons, he thought, surely the Lord's anointed stands right here. He reached for the horn of anointing oil that hung from his waist. But the voice of the Lord brought him up short, saying, "Do not consider his appearance or his height, for I have rejected him. The LORD does not look at the things people look at. People look at the outward appearance, but the LORD looks at the heart" (1 Samuel 16:7).

So Samuel continued. He reviewed six other sons of Jesse, and felt no confirmation that any of them were God's choice. Then Samuel learned that Jesse had one more son, the youngest, who was in the fields with the family's sheep herd. "Send for him," he said.

"We will not sit down until he arrives" (1 Samuel 16:11b).

When Samuel saw David he heard the Lord's voice say, "Rise and anoint him; this is the one."

So Samuel obeyed. In front of all of his brothers, the prophet anointed David as the king of Israel. And the Bible says, "from that day on the Spirit of the LORD came powerfully upon David" (1 Samuel 16:13b).

But there was just one problem. Saul still lived. Saul was still king. Saul still held sway in the land. Everyone who saw Samuel anoint the young shepherd understood that Saul had been deposed and David was God's chosen vessel. Though there was another king in the land, who could bring much evil on the people, the reign of the anointed one was coming, surely and soon.

Sound familiar?

Many years later, a Son of David appeared in the Judean landscape, a shepherd from Bethlehem. He approached John the Baptist, who had been announcing the coming of God's Anointed One, whose coming would usher in a new kingdom.

John protested when Jesus came to him for baptism. "I need to be baptized by you," he told Jesus. "Not the other way around."

But Jesus insisted. He explained, cryptically, that there was more going on than even a prophet like John realized at that moment. And, sure enough, when Jesus came up out of the water, the heavens opened, the Spirit of God descended on Jesus like a dove, and a voice from heaven said, "This is my beloved Son, my favored One."

It was more than a baptism. It was an anointing. There was another ruler still at large in the world, "the ruler of the kingdom of the air" (Ephesians 2:2), who would yet do much evil. But that ruler had been deposed. The Anointed One had come, and his reign was coming, surely and soon.

Leonard Sweet and Frank Viola write:

> From the very beginning, satan has sought to dethrone the Lord Jesus Christ from his rightful place. This is the essence of the battle that has raged through the ages. ... Thankfully, however, this battle has already been won. Jesus Christ has triumphed through the cross, and His church has entered into His victory. As a result, we are more than conquerors through him who loves us. Jesus Christ shall indeed reign over the universe,

satan will be cast out, and God's eternal purpose will be realized. However, in the interim, the battle over the earth continues to rage.[6]

As Martin Luther wrote in his hymn, "A Mighty Fortress," our "ancient foe" still seeks to "work us woe." But, though his power and craft are great, our Anointed One has defeated him and won the battle.

FROM THE BIBLE

So Samuel took the horn of oil and anointed him in the presence of his brothers, and from that day on the Spirit of the LORD came powerfully upon David.
—*1 Samuel 16:13*

I have found David my servant; with my sacred oil I have anointed him.
—*Psalm 89:20*

When all the people were being baptized, Jesus was baptized too. And as he was praying, heaven was opened and the Holy Spirit descended on him in bodily form like a dove. And a voice came from heaven: "You are my Son, whom I love; with you I am well pleased."
—*Luke 3:21–22*

"After this, God gave them judges until the time of Samuel the prophet. Then the people asked for a king, and he gave them Saul son of Kish, of the tribe of Benjamin, who ruled forty years. After removing Saul, he made David their king. God testified concerning him: 'I have found David son of Jesse, a man after my own heart; he will do everything I want him to do.'"
—*Acts 13:20–22*

FROM THE HEART

Lord Jesus, thank you for bringing your kingdom—to me, and mine, and to this hurting world in which I live. In Jesus' name, amen.

DID YOU KNOW?

Though David was anointed king of Israel by Samuel, it would be some years before his reign began. Only after Saul's death was David anointed king of Judah, the southern part of the kingdom (2 Samuel 2:4). Even then, David and his troops had to fight the house of Saul to consolidate the kingdom (2 Samuel 2, 3). He finally became king over Israel and Judah at the age of thirty (2 Samuel 5:4).

EXPERIENCE THE STORY: BRING THE KINGDOM

Look today for opportunities to "put feet to your prayer" for the Kingdom of God to come to fruition and fulfillment in your life and through your surroundings. Look for ways to do it symbolically and practically, in ways large and small (for example, helping a stranded motorist or paying attention to a child can be seen as the Kingdom of God being realized).

GO DEEPER

To study further, read the story of God's rejection of Saul as king and the anointing of David in 1 Samuel 15–16.

REFLECTION TIME

In the space below, jot down your thoughts in response to the questions:

- How can I more fully partake of the power that is available to me?
- Is there some submission or surrender I have yet to make?
- What can I do to more fully bring the Kingdom of God to the people I come into contact with regularly?

THE HEART OF A SHEPHERD

In those days, as in ours, certain occupations were considered more prestigious than others.

The three oldest brothers of David were soldiers in the army of King Saul. Fighting men. Warriors. But David occupied a position very typical for the youngest in the family. He tended his father's flocks. He worked as a shepherd. It was probably a job he had held for years. It was probably a responsibility he expected to hold for some time to come. And it was probably a career path with no prospect for advancement—only faithfulness.

One day, however, his father, Jesse, summoned David and told him to take provisions—an ephah of roasted grain, bread, and cheese—to his brothers in the Valley of Elah, and to bring back some news of how his brothers were doing. When David arrived, he learned that a huge Philistine warrior named Goliath of Gath had been coming out daily to the field of battle to taunt and challenge Saul's army.

David saw that Saul's warriors, including his own brothers, were cowed by the Philistine! No one volunteered to fight him, and when David made an issue of it, his brothers heaped ridicule on him. So David made a pest of himself in the Israelite camp, incredulously wondering why no one would step forward, until someone reported his activity to Saul.

David was brought before the king, who upbraided David for questioning the bravery of his men and undermining the morale of the troops. David answered, "Let no one lose heart on account of this Philistine; your servant will go and fight him" (1 Samuel 17:32).

Saul shook his head. "You!" he said. "No. You are little more than a boy, and this Goliath is a seasoned warrior."

What could David say? The king was right. He shot a silent prayer to heaven like a stone from a sling, and an instant later he had his answer. "I have been tending my father's sheep for years. Any time a lion or bear tried to carry off a lamb, I would defend the flock. I would kill the lion. I would kill the bear. The Lord was with me. He saved me from the paw of the lion and the paw of the bear, and he will do the same today. I will kill the Philistine."

David's resume may have been unimpressive. His experience may have been limited. But it turned out to have been exactly the preparation he needed, not only to risk his life and fight Goliath of Gath, but also to lead the people of Israel as their king.

Many years later, another man appeared in Israel. Another shepherd. He came into the camp of Israel, where the leaders of God's people were complacent and corrupt. He challenged them, and received only ridicule for his efforts. They scoffed at his resume (Mark 6:33). They doubted and derided him, calling him a Samaritan, and accusing him of being demon-possessed (John 8:48). But, like David, Jesus not only endured their abuse; he laid down his life for them, as the Good Shepherd:

> "I am the good shepherd. The good shepherd lays down his life for the sheep. The hired hand is not the shepherd and does not own the sheep. So when he sees the wolf coming, he abandons the sheep and runs away. Then the wolf attacks the flock and scatters it. The man runs away because he is a hired hand and cares nothing for the sheep.
>
> "I am the good shepherd; I know my sheep and my sheep know me—just as the Father knows me and I know the Father—and I lay down my life for the sheep. I have other sheep that are not of this sheep pen. I must bring them also. They too will listen to my voice, and there shall be one flock and one shepherd. The reason my Father loves me is that I lay down my life—only to take it up again. No one takes it from me, but I lay it down of my own accord. I have authority to lay it down and authority to take it up again. This command I received from my Father" (John 10:11–18).

FROM THE BIBLE

He chose David his servant and took him from the sheep pens;
from tending the sheep he brought him to be the shepherd of his
people Jacob, of Israel his inheritance.

And David shepherded them with integrity of heart; with skillful
hands he led them.
—*Psalm 78:70–72*

See, the Sovereign LORD comes with power, and he rules with a
mighty arm.

See, his reward is with him, and his recompense accompanies him.
He tends his flock like a shepherd:

He gathers the lambs in his arms and carries them close to his
heart; he gently leads those that have young.
—*Isaiah 40:10–11*

I will save my flock, and they will no longer be plundered. I will
judge between one sheep and another. I will place over them one
shepherd, my servant David, and he will tend them; he will tend
them and be their shepherd.
—*Ezekiel 34:22–23*

For "you were like sheep going astray," but now you have returned
to the Shepherd and Overseer of your souls.
—*1 Peter 2:25*

FROM THE HEART

Lord, you are my shepherd; I lack nothing that I really need. You
care for me and lead me. You restore and revive me. Even in the
darkest times, I don't have to be afraid, for I know you are there
with me, protecting me and comforting me. You provide my needs,
you pour out on me one blessing after another. Your goodness and
love—and constant presence—are all I need, now and forever.
Amen (Based on Psalm 23).

DID YOU KNOW?

Shepherding was a humble but necessary occupation in biblical times (and even today in that part of the world). Other shepherds in the Bible included Abel, Abraham, Lot, Isaac, Jacob, Moses, and, of course, the nameless Bethlehem shepherds to whom angels announced the birth of Jesus.

EXPERIENCE THE STORY: A MUSICAL MEDITATION

Using iTunes, Spotify, YouTube, or your own music collection, take a few minutes to listen to and meditate on a musical setting of Psalm 23 or Isaiah 40:11.

GO DEEPER

Using a concordance (in your Bible, in your library, or online), look up the many biblical references to shepherds; note how often the word is used to describe God—and godly leaders.

REFLECTION TIME

What are some of the ways Jesus shepherds me? (List them below):

_____

_____

_____

_____

_____

_____

_____

_____

_____

_____

THE CHAMPION

He was not a "Jack in the Beanstalk" kind of giant. But he was big—breathtakingly big.

Nearly all scholars agree that Goliath of Gath stood more than nine feet tall. A height not unheard of in our day or in ancient times. The Roman naturalist Pliny reported a man named Pusio and a woman named Secundilla who were over ten feet tall, and the historian Josephus wrote of a Jew who reached a height of over nine-and-a-half feet. In the twentieth century, an American named Robert Wadlow reached a height of eight feet eleven inches and was still growing when he died from an infection at the age of twenty-two.

But still. Goliath's size was prodigious and intimidating. Little wonder that the army of King Saul shrank from his challenges. Who in his right mind would volunteer to go up against a guy whose arms are more than four feet long? Who wants to fight someone who weighs more than four hundred pounds? There are just too many ways for a warrior of that stature to kill you. There are too many good reasons to take a pass.

Until a young man named David stepped forward. He was no bigger than others in the Israelite camp. He was downright puny next to King Saul. And he had far less battle experience than his warrior brothers. But Goliath had taunted them for forty days; David couldn't stomach a heathen Philistine defying and shaming the armies of the living God like that (1 Samuel 17:26).

So he volunteered to do battle with a vile, seemingly unbeatable enemy. He shunned the conventional tactics. He shrugged off the king's armor. He settled on a laughable weapon: a sling and a stone. He took the field of battle with no helmet, no armor, no shield, and no sword.

As David strode forward to meet him, Goliath couldn't believe his eyes:

> He looked David over and saw that he was little more than a boy, glowing with health and handsome, and he despised him. He said to David, "Am I a dog, that you come at me with sticks?" And the Philistine cursed David by his gods. "Come here," he said, "and I'll give your flesh to the birds and the wild animals!" (1 Samuel 17:42–44).

David may have swallowed hard. He may have had second thoughts. He may have prayed for a way out. We really don't know. But we do know that he didn't run. He set his face like flint and walked toward the enemy.

> David said to the Philistine, "You come against me with sword and spear and javelin, but I come against you in the name of the LORD Almighty, the God of the armies of Israel, whom you have defied. This day the LORD will deliver you into my hands, and I'll strike you down and cut off your head. This very day I will give the carcasses of the Philistine army to the birds and the wild animals, and the whole world will know that there is a God in Israel. All those gathered here will know that it is not by sword or spear that the LORD saves; for the battle is the LORD's, and he will give all of you into our hands" (1 Samuel 17:45–47).

Then David ran. But he ran toward Goliath. He loaded a stone into his sling and sent it to its mark. It struck Goliath of Gath above his eyes, with such force that it embedded in his skin. And the warrior dropped to the ground. David leaped into his advantage, picked up Goliath's own sword, and finished the job. He won the contest. He won the battle. He won a shocking victory by unconventional means against a seemingly unbeatable foe.

In doing so, David again foreshadowed the coming of Jesus. The enemy Jesus faced was more formidable. The stakes were much higher. His burden was much greater.

He shunned the conventional tactics. He took the field of battle virtually naked. Silent. Defenseless. We know he prayed for a way out (Mark 14:35–36). We know also that he set his face like flint and faced his task resolutely (Luke 9:51). And, like David, he emerged victorious. David killed Goliath with a stone in a valley; Jesus beat the Devil with a stick—a cross on a hill.

FROM THE BIBLE

So David triumphed over the Philistine with a sling and a stone; without a sword in his hand he struck down the Philistine and killed him.
—*1 Samuel 17:50*

He took his life in his hands when he killed the Philistine. The LORD won a great victory for all Israel, and you saw it and were glad.
—*1 Samuel 19:5*

Because the Sovereign LORD helps me, I will not be disgraced. Therefore have I set my face like flint, and I know I will not be put to shame.
—*Isaiah 50:7*

When the time was coming near for Jesus to depart, he was determined to go to Jerusalem.
—*Luke 9:51 (NCV)*

When you were dead in your sins and in the uncircumcision of your flesh, God made you alive with Christ. He forgave us all our sins, having canceled the charge of our legal indebtedness, which stood against us and condemned us; he has taken it away, nailing it to the cross. And having disarmed the powers and authorities, he made a public spectacle of them, triumphing over them by the cross.
—*Colossians 2:13–15*

FROM THE HEART

Lord Jesus, Son of David, I praise you for your faithfulness and courage in facing all that you endured in your Passion. I praise you for your victory over sin, death, and the devil. I praise you for having disarmed all the powers and authorities, for making a public spectacle of them, and for triumphing over them by the cross. In Jesus' name, amen.

DID YOU KNOW?

Aren Maeir of Bar-Ilan University in Israel has been leading an archaeological excavation of the Philistine city of Gath, the hometown of Goliath, in recent years. It was a prominent town on the border of Philistia and Israel.

EXPERIENCE THE STORY: ONE SMOOTH STONE

Carry a stone or a stick in your pocket, purse, or wallet today. Every time you see it or touch it, say a quick prayer of thanks for Jesus' victory over the enemy of your soul.

GO DEEPER

For further study, read the full account of David and Goliath in 1 Samuel 17.

REFLECTION TIME

Martin Luther may have had the birth of Jesus, the Incarnate Word of God, in mind when he wrote these lines in his hymn, "A Mighty Fortress":

> And though this world, with devils filled, should threaten to undo us,
> We will not fear, for God hath willed His truth to triumph through us:
> The Prince of Darkness grim, we tremble not for him;
> His rage we can endure, for lo, his doom is sure,
> One little word shall fell him.

As David felled the giant with a tiny stone, God sent a "little word," the Eternal Word in infant form, to fell the Prince of Darkness. Take a few moments to ponder the ways in which God has "felled" the work of the devil in your heart and life.

Reading the stories of the Bible as we've been doing these past two weeks should lead to at least one nearly inescapable conclusion: Jesus shows up repeatedly.

We may know, theologically speaking, that the eternal Word of God was present in the Creation and the Exodus and the Conquest of Canaan, and so on. We may sometimes recognize foreshadowing in the stories of the Binding of Isaac and the Passover. But it is another thing entirely to see how our Lord and his salvation are prefigured in story after story. It can be a wonderful thing to contemplate how throughout biblical history, our salvation was planned and prepared for in so many other stories.

One of the messages we are clearly intended to take to heart is our Lord's willingness—determination, even—to ransom every human heart from slavery, as Rahab was rescued from Jericho and the Israelites from servitude to the Philistines. It should also be marvelously clear that he will use all means necessary to lead us to freedom—as he used a prostitute, a mercurial strongman, and an easily overlooked shepherd boy named David.

As you read and meditate on these stories, let it become apparent to you that Jesus is also likely to reveal himself in your story. Think back on the highs and lows of your life; do you see him there? Can you identify his presence and work in things that may not have seemed important at the time? Are there hints and signs that become clearer as you look back, like the scarlet rope Rahab hung in the window?

The Bible says, "It is for freedom that Christ has set us free" (Galatians 5:1). In other words, if you have been freed from sin, death, guilt, and shame by the work of Jesus Christ, he intends for you to remain free—to live free. And to show others around you what freedom looks like.

WEEK TWO: SMALL-GROUP STUDY AND DISCUSSION QUESTIONS

Below is a complete list of small-group study and discussion questions for small groups that use this guidebook in conjunction with *The Bible 30-Day Experience DVD Study.* In order to stay within the time limits of your small-group meeting, your small-group leader will choose what questions he or she wants your group to focus on. You will want to bring this guidebook with you to your small group or class.

1. Open in prayer.

2. Go around the room asking everyone to briefly answer this question: "What is the biggest challenge you've ever faced?"

3. Watch video: "David and Goliath."

4. Question: "As you watched the video, what did you find most interesting or inspiring?"

5. Question: "If you had been there that day, say as one of Israel's soldiers, what do you think you would have been thinking or feeling as Goliath came out to taunt Saul and his troops?"

6. Read 1 Samuel 17:1–11, 32–51.

7. Question: "What did Goliath say (in the video and in verse 9) would happen if he defeated an Israelite champion? And what would happen if an Israelite champion defeated him?"

8. Question: "Verses 12–31, though we didn't read them, make it clear that David was no soldier. Since he had no training or experience in warfare, what reason did he give King Saul (in vv. 36–37) to let him fight Goliath?"

9. Question: "Reread David's speech to Goliath in verses 45–47. What do you think of David's words? Were they bluster? A response to Goliath's taunts? Did he think they would scare Goliath? Or was something else going on?"

10. Question: "According to verses 49–51, what killed Goliath—David's stone or Goliath's own sword?"

11. Question: "Think back to the terms of battle, as defined by Goliath in verse 9; David's victory made him a hero, of course—but what did his triumph mean for the nation of Israel?"

12. Question: "Can you think of any ways in which David's confrontation with Goliath parallels Jesus taking on sin, Satan, and death on the cross?"

13. Question: "David saved Israel that day from slavery to the Philistines. Jesus' victory on the cross saved us from slavery to sin. What do you think that means for us in practical terms?" (HINT: What did the Israelites do after Goliath was killed? [See 1 Samuel 17:52ff])

14. Question: "What sorts of 'giants' are you facing right now?"

15. Question: "What are some ways you can apply this story and its lessons to your life this week?"

16. Any other questions or comments?

17. Close in prayer.

WEEK THREE THEME:

FROM VICTIM TO VICTOR

MAIN MESSAGE POINT:

THE "GREAT SALVATION" (HEBREWS 2:3) GOD PROVIDES MEANS THAT I AM NO LONGER A VICTIM OF SIN AND CIRCUMSTANCE, BUT CAN BE VICTORIOUS THROUGH HIM WHO LOVES ME.

THIS WEEK'S MEMORY VERSE:

"IN ALL THESE THINGS, WE ARE MORE THAN CONQUERORS THROUGH HIM WHO LOVED US."
—ROMANS 8:37

THE REVEALED WORD

Daniel was just one among many.

Babylon's King Nebuchadnezzar, the most powerful man in the world, had assembled a royal court of advisors, astrologers, and sorcerers to counsel him in the many weighty decisions he faced as the ruler of a vast kingdom that stretched from the Mediterranean Sea in the west to the Persian Gulf in the east, and from the Taurus Mountains (present-day southern Turkey) in the north to the Arabian Peninsula in the south. For such a ruler, the smallest decision can have far-reaching consequences. So, when Nebuchadnezzar woke one morning from a strange and disturbing dream, he summoned his court officials—Daniel among them—to interpret the dream.

There was just one problem: He would not describe the dream to them. After all, if they truly possessed supernatural powers, they should be able to figure out what the king dreamed and interpret it for him. In fact, he said if no one in his court did what he asked, they would all be summarily executed.

Understandably, the court officials protested.

"No one can do what the king asks!" they said.

"It's impossible!"

"It's unprecedented!"

"It's unreasonable!"

But Nebuchadnezzar wouldn't budge. So the order went out. They were all to be executed.

So Daniel, one of many exiles from Jerusalem who had been brought to Nebuchadnezzar's capital city against his will, prayed. He asked his closest friends—fellow exiles—to pray, too. Nothing like a death threat to spark a prayer meeting.

It worked. That night, God revealed the king's dream to Daniel in a vision. So Daniel requested an audience with the king.

The king asked Daniel (also called Belteshazzar), "Are you able to tell me what I saw in my dream and interpret it?"

Daniel replied, "No wise man, enchanter, magician or diviner can explain to the king the mystery he has asked about, but there is a God in heaven who reveals mysteries. He has shown King Nebuchadnezzar what will happen in days to come" (Daniel 2:26–28).

Daniel went on to give the king a full description and interpretation of the dream, as God had revealed it to Daniel—thus not only saving Daniel and his friends from becoming victims of a despot's whims, but also distinguishing Daniel from all the other court officials as someone with a unique connection to the God of Heaven. It would not be the last time God sent his Word through Daniel. It was not the last time God used Daniel to untangle mysteries for men.

Hundreds of years later, a man named John would take pen in hand to tell the story of Jesus, and would describe it this way:

In the beginning was the Word, and the Word was with God, and the Word was God. He was with God in the beginning. Through him all things were made; without him nothing was made that has been made. In him was life, and that life was the light of all mankind. The light shines in the darkness, and the darkness has not overcome it (John 1:1–5).

Daniel received a word from God that not only saved his neck—it reversed his fate; it changed him from victim to victor. It was a token of a day in the future when the Father revealed the Eternal Word to all humanity, and gave every one of us the same chance Daniel had—to escape death, to apprehend mysteries, and to be transformed from victim to victor.

It is no coincidence—no mere turn of phrase—that Jesus is referred to by John as "the Word of God." It reveals Jesus as far more than the English translation makes possible. He is the *Logos*, the expression, the revelation, the eloquence, the wisdom, and the testimony of God, in whom the fullness of the Godhead is displayed. And, as Daniel's story foreshadows, it is from Christ alone that we can receive the knowledge that saves, and that can transform us from victims to victors.

FROM THE BIBLE

During the night the mystery was revealed to Daniel in a vision. Then Daniel praised the God of heaven and said:

"Praise be to the name of God for ever and ever; wisdom and power are his.

He changes times and seasons; he deposes kings and raises up others.

He gives wisdom to the wise and knowledge to the discerning.

He reveals deep and hidden things; he knows what lies in darkness,

and light dwells with him.

I thank and praise you, God of my ancestors:

You have given me wisdom and power, you have made known to me what we asked of you, you have made known to us the dream of the king."

—Daniel 2:19–23

The Word became flesh and made his dwelling among us. We have seen his glory, the glory of the one and only Son, who came from the Father, full of grace and truth.

—John 1:14

Although I am less than the least of all the Lord's people, this grace was given me: to preach to the Gentiles the boundless riches of Christ, and to make plain to everyone the administration of this mystery, which for ages past was kept hidden in God, who created all things. His intent was that now, through the church, the manifold wisdom of God should be made known to the rulers and authorities in the heavenly realms, according to his eternal purpose that he accomplished in Christ Jesus our Lord.

—Ephesians 3:8–11

FROM THE HEART

Lord God, I praise your name; wisdom and power are yours. You change times and seasons; you depose kings and raise up others. You give wisdom to the wise and knowledge to the discerning. You reveal deep and hidden things; you know what lies in darkness, and light dwells with you. Grant me the wisdom to look to you for wisdom! Help me to walk in the light you give me, and to live victoriously by trusting in you. In Jesus' name, amen.

DID YOU KNOW?

God often spoke to people through dreams in the Bible. Abimelech, king of Gerar, learned in a dream that Sarah was really Abraham's wife (Genesis 20:1–7). Jacob had a dream of a ladder (or staircase) reaching to heaven (Genesis 28:10–17). God gave Joseph the ability to interpret dreams, which resulted in Joseph's promotion to second-in-command in Egypt (Genesis 40–41). Daniel would certainly have known these stories, and that knowledge may have inspired him to pray for the ability to interpret Nebuchadnezzar's dream.

EXPERIENCE THE STORY: ENLIST PRAYER PARTNERS

When Daniel faced a seemingly impossible situation, he enlisted three friends to pray with him and for him. If you don't already have prayer partners, write below the names of two or three friends you could enlist as prayer partners, and contact them before the end of the day to ask if they would pray with you and for you (see the Reflection Time below for a possible topic of prayer).

GO DEEPER

For further study, compare the story of Nebuchadnezzar's dream in Daniel 2 with the account of Pharaoh's dreams in Genesis 41.

REFLECTION TIME

Three areas in which I could use wisdom from the Word of God today:

1. _____

2. _____

3. _____

THE FOURTH MAN

It would have been easy for them to feel sorry for themselves.

After all, Shadrach, Meshach, and Abednego were minding their own business. They were not trying to stir up trouble. They meant no disrespect.

But when King Nebuchadnezzar erected a massive gold statue and commanded everyone in his kingdom to worship before it, they had to abstain, in spite of the fact that the king had decreed that anyone who refused to worship the image would be thrown into a blazing furnace and burned alive. They were Jews. They worshiped God, the one God, and him alone.

Unfortunately, there were some people in Nebuchadnezzar's court who saw an opportunity. They reported Shadrach, Meshach, and Abednego to the king.

So Nebuchadnezzar summoned them to appear before him:

> And Nebuchadnezzar said to them, "Is it true, Shadrach, Meshach and Abednego, that you do not serve my gods or worship the image of gold I have set up? Now when you hear the sound of the horn, flute, zither, lyre, harp, pipe and all kinds of music, if you are ready to fall down and worship the image I made, very good. But if you do not worship it, you will be thrown immediately into a blazing furnace. Then what god will be able to rescue you from my hand?" (Daniel 3:14–15).

It was a horrible predicament. It was so unfair. They were being singled out for mistreatment. They were the victims of a vicious conspiracy. But they didn't whine or complain. They didn't protest.

They didn't denounce the people who snitched on them.

> Shadrach, Meshach and Abednego replied to him, "King Nebuchadnezzar, we do not need to defend ourselves before you in this matter. If we are thrown into the blazing furnace, the God we serve is able to deliver us from it, and he will deliver us from Your Majesty's hand. But even if he does not, we want you to know, Your Majesty, that we will not serve your gods or worship the image of gold you have set up" (Daniel 3:16-18).

You probably know what happened next. They were thrown into the furnace, and Nebuchadnezzar sat back to watch them burn. But they didn't. They were not consumed by the flames. They actually walked around inside the furnace, and seemed unharmed, and no longer bound. Moreover, as the king watched, another form appeared with them in the flames. A fourth man. Someone that looked to the king like "a son of the gods!" (Daniel 3:25, NASB).

Moments later, Nebuchadnezzar called to Shadrach, Meshach, and Abednego. He summoned them out of the furnace and they came. The king and his advisors crowded around and gawked at the three friends in amazement. They were unharmed. Their hair wasn't even singed. Their clothes didn't even smell like smoke!

They had entered the furnace as victims; they emerged victorious. They entered as three friends; they were joined by a fourth. They entered under a cloud of accusation; soon after, they were exalted to even higher government positions than before.

The Bible never explains the "fourth man" in the furnace. The book of Daniel doesn't elaborate on the identity of the one who looked like "a son of the gods." Perhaps it's because it doesn't need explaining. Maybe it is just that obvious. After all, God had spoken to his people—before they were exiled from Jerusalem—through the prophet Isaiah:

> When you pass through the waters,
> I will be with you; and when you pass through the rivers, they will not sweep over you.
> When you walk through the fire, you will not be burned; the flames will not set you ablaze (Isaiah 43:2).

Perhaps Jesus meant for his followers to remember that promise and picture that Babylonian furnace when he told them, "Where two or three gather in my name, there am I with them" (Matthew 18:20), or maybe not. In any case, it certainly applies. If One like the Son of God could show up in a blazing-hot furnace for three men named Shadrach, Meshach, and Abednego, and deliver them from evil and reverse their fortunes, can he not be with you—wherever you are and whatever your need?

FROM THE BIBLE

[Nebuchadnezzar] said, "Look! I see four men walking around in the fire, unbound and unharmed, and the fourth looks like a son of the gods."
—*Daniel 3:25*

"I will save you from the hands of the wicked and deliver you from the grasp of the cruel."
—*Jeremiah 15:21*

"And surely I am with you always, to the very end of the age."
—*Matthew 28:20*

FROM THE HEART

Lord Jesus, as you were with Shadrach, Meshach, and Abednego in the fiery furnace, thank you that you are with me in the trials that come my way. Help me to stand firm in the face of accusation and persecution, and let me emerge from every trial not as a victim but victorious in you. In Jesus' name, amen.

DID YOU KNOW?

Daniel 3:22 contains an interesting detail: "The king's command was so urgent and the furnace so hot that the flames of the fire killed the soldiers who took up Shadrach, Meshach and Abednego." That verse adds emphasis to God's deliverance of his three Hebrew servants. If the fire was hot enough to kill even those who, while staying outside the furnace, cast the victims into the fire, there could certainly have been no natural expectation that anyone could survive the flames—yet not even the three friends' clothes or hair were destroyed!

EXPERIENCE THE STORY: REMEMBER A PROMISE

Commit the second part of Isaiah 43:2 to memory today ("when you walk through the fire, you will not be burned; the flames will not set you ablaze"), and repeat it to yourself whenever you face difficult trials. Alternately: Copy the verse onto a piece of paper and keep it with you.

GO DEEPER

For further study, read the full account of the three friends in the furnace in Daniel 3.

REFLECTION TIME

In the space provided below, reflect on:

- One time in my life when I felt like I walked through the fire but was not consumed.
- One time in my life when Jesus' promise to be with me always was fulfilled.
- One time in my life when God's presence with me was noticed by someone nearby.

IN THE HANDS OF BETRAYERS

Who is the most faithful person you know? The most dependable? The one person who can be trusted to do the right thing in every circumstance?

In the kingdom of Nebuchadnezzar, that person was Daniel. When Belshazzar became king of Babylon, that person was still Daniel. When Darius the Mede took over, that person was, you guessed it, Daniel.

But such faithfulness sometimes arouses opposition, jealousy, and even hatred. And such was the case with Daniel. The Bible says:

> Daniel so distinguished himself among the administrators and the satraps by his exceptional qualities that the king planned to set him over the whole kingdom. At this, the administrators and the satraps tried to find grounds for charges against Daniel in his conduct of government affairs, but they were unable to do so. They could find no corruption in him, because he was trustworthy and neither corrupt nor negligent. Finally these men said, "We will never find any basis for charges against this man Daniel unless it has something to do with the law of his God" (Daniel 6:3–5).

Stop right there. Did you catch that? Daniel was so blameless that his enemies figured the only way they could ever attack him would be to concoct charges related to his faith. Bible scholar Matthew Henry said, "It is an excellent thing, and much for the glory of God, when those who profess religion conduct themselves so inoffensively in their whole conversation that their most watchful spiteful enemies may find no occasion of blaming them, save only in the matters of their God, in which they walk according to their consciences."[7]

That was certainly the case with Daniel. So his enemies executed an elaborate plan. First, they persuaded Darius to decree a thirty-day period in which everyone in the kingdom was required to worship and pray only to the king himself. Once the decree was in place, they watched Daniel, who didn't disappoint them; he continued his former habit of praying to God three times a day. So the conspirators scurried off to the king, reminded him of his decree, and told him that no less a person than Daniel had run afoul of the law.

The plot worked. Not only was Daniel betrayed; the king himself was confined by his own laws. Darius tried everything he could think of to save Daniel, to no avail. He issued the order for Daniel to be led away to judgment.

In the story of Daniel can be found intimations of another story:

- Daniel was a righteous man—so much so that he could refer to himself as "innocent" in his actions toward King Darius without fear of contradiction (Daniel 6:22). Jesus was utterly without sin (1 Peter 2:22), blameless before God and man.
- Daniel was targeted by other officials because he had distinguished himself and gained the favor and trust of the king. Jesus was targeted by the religious authorities of his day because he was becoming too popular with the common people (John 11:48, 12:19).
- Daniel was betrayed by other government officials who were jealous of his success. Jesus was betrayed by a friend, with whom he broke bread and shared his life (John 13:18).

"Search the Scriptures …" Jesus said. "The Scriptures point to me!" (John 5:39, NLT). From the first pages of Genesis through the prophecy of Malachi—and beyond—the Hebrew Scriptures tell the story of Jesus in sign and symbol, in story and parable. And they do so with good reason.

Have you ever been targeted for ill treatment? Have you ever been wrongly accused? Have you ever felt betrayed? Have you ever stood up for what is right, only to be misunderstood and abused? If you have, then guess what: Jesus saw it. He experienced it, not only in his Passion, but in your agony as well. He was there in your agony, as he was prefigured in Daniel's experience. And in such times, he will walk with you and find a way to soothe and even deliver you in your darkest nights.

FROM THE BIBLE

Finally these men said, "We will never find any basis for charges against this man Daniel unless it has something to do with the law of his God."
—*Daniel 6:5*

Now when Daniel learned that the decree had been published, he went home to his upstairs room where the windows opened toward Jerusalem. Three times a day he got down on his knees and prayed, giving thanks to his God, just as he had done before.
—*Daniel 6:10*

Keeping a close watch on him, they sent spies, who pretended to be sincere. They hoped to catch Jesus in something he said, so that they might hand him over to the power and authority of the governor.
—*Luke 20:20*

Live such good lives among the pagans that, though they accuse you of doing wrong, they may see your good deeds and glorify God on the day he visits us.
—*1 Peter 2:12*

FROM THE HEART

Gracious Lord, thank you for the Scriptures, which testify so beautifully of Jesus. Help me, like Daniel and like Jesus, to be strong in the face of accusation and persecution. Help me to conduct myself so inoffensively in all I do that my most watchful and spiteful enemies may find nothing to blame, except in matters touching on my faithfulness to you. In Jesus' name, amen.

DID YOU KNOW?

Skeptics once claimed that the book of Daniel was of much later authorship than the time of the events it describes, meaning Daniel couldn't have written the book. Some suggested it was written as late as the second century BC. However, when the Dead Sea Scrolls were discovered in 1947, a copy of Daniel was among them. Since the Dead Sea Scrolls dated to the second century BC and the book of Daniel appeared to have been reverenced as Scripture by the community that preserved the scrolls, the theories of late authorship had to be revised.

EXPERIENCE THE STORY: PRAY THREE TIMES TODAY

Set the alarm on your cell phone, place reminders in your calendar, or find some other way to jog your memory to pray, like Daniel, three times today. It doesn't have to be a long time of prayer. Just take a few moments at three separate times in your day to turn your thoughts and your voice toward heaven.

GO DEEPER

For further study, read the full account of the scheme to trap Daniel in Daniel 6.

REFLECTION TIME

Take some time to reflect on these questions, and write any responses below:
- How do I usually respond to ill treatment?
- Does my typical response make things better? Worse?
- How can I respond in the future in ways that will glorify God?

THE RIGHTEOUS ACCUSED

When King Darius issued a decree that his subjects should pray only to him for a period of thirty days (Daniel 6:1–9), we know that Daniel "went home to his upstairs room ... [and] got down on his knees and prayed, giving thanks to his God, just as he had done before" (Daniel 6:10b). He was faithful and obedient.

But we don't know if he was calm and unafraid.

We may picture him serenely returning to his lodgings in the royal palace. Serenely opening his windows, serenely kneeling, and serenely praying.

Is that how you would react, knowing that your obedience to God could result in a death sentence? Or would your steps be a little heavier on your way to your room? Would your hand tremble as you opened the window? Would you swallow hard as you knelt? Would you hold your breath for a moment before you began praying?

Daniel may have felt a lot more like that as he dropped to his knees on that fateful day in Babylon. He may even have struggled in prayer in much the same way Jesus did in the Garden of Gethsemane:

> They went to a place called Gethsemane, and Jesus said to his disciples, "Sit here while I pray." He took Peter, James and John along with him, and he began to be deeply distressed and troubled. "My soul is overwhelmed with sorrow to the point of death," he said to them. "Stay here and keep watch."
>
> Going a little farther, he fell to the ground and prayed that if possible the hour might pass from him. "Abba, Father," he

said, "everything is possible for you. Take this cup from me. Yet not what I will, but what you will."

Then he returned to his disciples and found them sleeping. "Simon," he said to Peter, "are you asleep? Couldn't you keep watch for one hour? Watch and pray so that you will not fall into temptation. The spirit is willing, but the flesh is weak."

Once more he went away and prayed the same thing. When he came back, he again found them sleeping, because their eyes were heavy. They did not know what to say to him.

Returning the third time, he said to them, "Are you still sleeping and resting? Enough! The hour has come. Look, the Son of Man is delivered into the hands of sinners. Rise! Let us go! Here comes my betrayer!" (Mark 14:32–42).

Both Daniel and Jesus persevered and obeyed, though they knew they faced a death sentence. We don't know how much Daniel knew about the cost of his obedience, but Jesus knew well—painfully well—what lay ahead of him.

Both Daniel and Jesus were betrayed, though they had done no wrong. And that is far from the only way that Daniel's story prefigures Jesus' Passion.

Daniel was trapped by the work of a group of conspirators who were determined to eliminate him. Similarly, the Pharisees and Sadducees tried repeatedly to trap Jesus and concoct grounds to arrest him (Matthew 16:1, John 8:6, etc.).

Daniel was arrested and condemned, even though the king wanted badly to find a way to release him. Jesus was framed by a group of conspirators who were determined to eliminate him. Jesus, of course, was arrested by the chief priests and scribes and taken to Pilate, who decreed three times that he found no fault in Jesus (John 18:38, 19:4, 19:6). In fact, the Gospel writer Matthew records:

When Pilate saw that he was getting nowhere, but that instead an uproar was starting, he took water and washed his hands in front of the crowd. "I am innocent of this man's blood," he said. "It is your responsibility!" (Matthew 27:24).

Neither Pilate nor Darius succeeded in their efforts; both were hemmed in by legal and political considerations.

But it didn't matter in the end. Daniel was thrown to the lions; Jesus was crucified by the Romans. Neither, however, was abandoned to the grave (Psalm 16:10): When King Darius went to the lions' den in the morning, he found Daniel—miraculously—alive, a preview of that Resurrection Sunday when Mary Magdalene went to the tomb of Jesus and heard the angel say, "He is not here; he has risen!" (Luke 24:6).

FROM THE BIBLE

Now when Daniel learned that the decree had been published, he went home to his upstairs room where the windows opened toward Jerusalem. Three times a day he got down on his knees and prayed, giving thanks to his God, just as he had done before.
—*Daniel 6:10*

The Pharisees and Sadducees came to Jesus and tested him by asking him to show them a sign from heaven.
—Matthew 16:1

They were using this question as a trap, in order to have a basis for accusing him.
—*John 8:6*

The administrators and the satraps tried to find grounds for charges against Daniel in his conduct of government affairs, but they were unable to do so.
—*Daniel 6:4*

Then Pilate announced to the chief priests and the crowd, "I find no basis for a charge against this man."
—*Luke 23:4*

When Daniel was lifted from the den, no wound was found on him, because he had trusted in his God.
—*Daniel 6:23b*

FROM THE HEART

Lord God Almighty, what forethought and foresight you showed, all through history, in weaving the redemption story throughout Scripture! Thank you for reminding me through Daniel's story of the Father's faithfulness to both him and to Jesus in his Passion. Thank you that their story has become a part of my story. In Jesus' name, amen.

DID YOU KNOW?

Daniel would have been a teenager when he was taken, with other captives, to Babylon. Accordingly, he would have been in his eighties when he was sent into the lions' den.

EXPERIENCE THE STORY: OPEN A WINDOW

The Bible says that when Daniel learned of the king's decree, he went to his room, opened a window, and prayed. Open a window— in your car, office, home, etc.—as a way of reminding yourself that God is with you, to comfort and defend you, as he was with Daniel in far-off Babylon. (If your climate or other circumstances make this impractical, you can also open a drawer or cupboard door instead).

GO DEEPER

For further study, compare the description of Daniel's prayer habits with the following Scripture passages: Psalm 55:17, Psalm 92:1–2, Psalm 141:2, and Matthew 6:6.

REFLECTION TIME

Take some time to reflect on these questions below:
- If prayer suddenly became illegal, would my habits be enough to convict me?
- Do I believe anything so strongly that I would risk my life for it?
- Am I being challenged in some way to stand by my convictions?

THE ANGELIC ANNOUNCEMENT

Few pieces of mail are more welcome these days than a birth announcement.

"It's a boy!"

"It's a girl!"

"It's TWINS!"

That is one of the few things that haven't changed in the last several thousand years.

But some announcements are even more welcome than that.

An angel—or perhaps even the Lord himself, in the company of two angels—appeared at Mamre one day and announced that Abraham's ninety-year-old wife would have a son in the next year. Sarah overheard the announcement and laughed (Genesis 18:12). But God himself had the last laugh; when the child was born the following year, he was named Isaac—which means "he laughs."

Many centuries later, when the people of Israel were cruelly oppressed by the Philistines, a man named Manoah had a wife who was unable to conceive a child. Then one day, an angel appeared to her and told her she would not only become pregnant, but would give birth to a son, which was the preferred outcome in those days, especially for a firstborn child. The angel told her that her child was to be raised as a Nazirite, which meant that from the day of his birth his hair would never be cut. The angel's words were fulfilled, and Manoah's wife gave birth to Samson, who famously delivered Israel from subjection to the Philistines.

Nearly a millennium later, an angel named Gabriel appeared to a man named Zechariah, who was a priest of God serving at the Temple in Jerusalem. Although Zechariah and his wife, Elizabeth, were "righteous in the sight of God" (Luke 1:6), they had never been blessed with children, and both had become too old to even hope for a child. That was when an angel appeared to Zechariah as he entered the Temple to burn incense before the Lord. The angel announced that Elizabeth would bear a son, who was to be named John, and who would "bring back many of the people of Israel to the Lord their God" (Luke 1:16).

All those angelic announcements, however, were prologue to the birth announcement the world awaited:

> In the sixth month of Elizabeth's pregnancy, God sent the angel Gabriel to Nazareth, a town in Galilee, to a virgin pledged to be married to a man named Joseph, a descendant of David. The virgin's name was Mary. The angel went to her and said, "Greetings, you who are highly favored! The Lord is with you." Mary was greatly troubled at his words and wondered what kind of greeting this might be. But the angel said to her, "Do not be afraid, Mary; you have found favor with God. You will conceive and give birth to a son, and you are to call him Jesus. He will be great and will be called the Son of the Most High. The Lord God will give him the throne of his father David, and he will reign over Jacob's descendants forever; his kingdom will never end."
> "How will this be," Mary asked the angel, "since I am a virgin?"
> The angel answered, "The Holy Spirit will come on you, and the power of the Most High will overshadow you. So the holy one to be born will be called the Son of God. Even Elizabeth your relative is going to have a child in her old age, and she who was said to be unable to conceive is in her sixth month. For no word from God will ever fail."
> "I am the Lord's servant," Mary answered. "May your word to me be fulfilled." Then the angel left her (Luke 1:26–38).

That angelic announcement heralded the birth of one who would fulfill and surpass all the promise and greatness of Isaac, Samson, and John the Baptist put together. He would establish the New

Israel, as Isaac had founded the old. He would deliver the oppressed and set the captives free (Isaiah 61:1), more than the strength of a thousand Samsons could have achieved. And he would bring a sinful and hurting humanity to the Lord their God, and "bestow on them a crown of beauty instead of ashes, the oil of joy instead of mourning, and a garment of praise instead of a spirit of despair" (Isaiah 61:3a).

FROM THE BIBLE

For to us a child is born, to us a son is given, and the government will be on his shoulders.

And he will be called Wonderful Counselor, Mighty God, Everlasting Father, Prince of Peace.

Of the greatness of his government and peace there will be no end. He will reign on David's throne and over his kingdom, establishing and upholding it with justice and righteousness from that time on and forever.

The zeal of the Lord Almighty will accomplish this.
—*Isaiah 9:6–7*

The Spirit of the Sovereign Lord is on me, because the Lord has anointed me

to proclaim good news to the poor.
He has sent me to bind up the brokenhearted, to proclaim freedom for the captives

and release from darkness for the prisoners, to proclaim the year of the Lord's favor

and the day of vengeance of our God, to comfort all who mourn, and provide for those who grieve in Zion—to bestow on them a crown of beauty instead of ashes, the oil of joy instead of mourning, and a garment of praise instead of a spirit of despair.

They will be called oaks of righteousness, a planting of the Lord for the display of his splendor.
—*Isaiah 9:6–7*

FROM THE HEART

Lord Jesus, by faith I thank you for doing for me and all whom I love what your Incarnation made possible. Thank you for healing our hearts, freeing us from any and all bondage, dispelling our darkness, and comforting and providing for us. Thank you for bestowing a crown of beauty for ashes, the oil of joy instead of mourning, and a garment of praise instead of a spirit of despair. In Jesus' name, amen.

DID YOU KNOW?

The Gospel of Luke identifies the angel who appeared to Mary to announce Jesus' birth as Gabriel (who identified himself to Zechariah, the father of John the Baptist, as the one who stands in the presence of God). However, Matthew never mentions the name of the angel who appeared to Joseph.

EXPERIENCE THE STORY:
PRAY THE MARY PRAYER

Though your circumstances probably won't compare to the news the angel Gabriel imparted when he announced the life-changing news of Jesus' impending birth to Mary, seize every opportunity today to echo her prayer nonetheless: "I am the Lord's servant. ... May your word be fulfilled in me."

GO DEEPER

For further study, compare the angelic announcements in Matthew 1:18–25, 2:13–14, and 2:19–21 with the angelic announcements in Luke 1:5–38.

REFLECTION TIME

Reflect on one or more of these questions below. How has the coming of Jesus already:
- healed my heart?
- freed me from bondage?
- dispelled my darkness?
- comforted me in sorrow?
- provided beauty for ashes, joy instead of mourning, and praise instead of despair?

THE LIFTER OF THE CURSE

Paradise started to slip from her hands when she heard those words: "Did God really say, 'You must not eat from any tree in the garden'?" (Genesis 3:1).

She felt confused. She tried to remember what God had said, as her husband had told her. She hesitated. She doubted. She tried to refute what the shimmering serpent said, but she got it only partly right.

It was safe to say that she should never have crept closer to the tree and inspected the fruit. She saw that it was good for food. She saw that it was pleasing to the eye. And she took to heart the serpent's claim that it was also desirable for gaining wisdom. Being deceived by the devil's craftiness she plucked it from the tree and ate. Her husband, who was with her, also ate. This direct disobedience of God's command was a choice that thereafter brought them—and everyone they loved—nothing but sorrow and death.

Many generations later, a Second Adam was born. Not into a pristine garden, but into a smelly stable. Perfection surrounded by filth. The first Adam inhaled the breath of life and became a living soul; the Second Adam, was a life-giving spirit (1 Corinthians 15:45). Upon being baptized in the Jordan River, He saw the heavens open and the Spirit of God descend on him like a dove. The first Adam received the Creator's command about the Tree of Good and Evil; the Second Adam received the Father's blessing: "This is my Son, whom I love; with him I am well pleased" (Matthew 3:17).

"Then," the Bible says, "Jesus was led by the Spirit into the wilderness to be tempted by the devil" (Matthew 4:1). The Second Adam would not be tempted in a garden, but in a desert. Rather than partake of trees that were "good for food" (Genesis 2:9), he fasted. He had no "bone of my bones and flesh of my flesh" to keep him company; he was alone.

After forty days of solitude, hunger, and thirst, "The tempter came to him and said, "If you are the Son of God, tell these stones to become bread" (Matthew 4:3). Jesus answered, "It is written: 'Man shall not live on bread alone, but on every word that comes from the mouth of God" (Matthew 4:4).

It didn't end there. The tempter is nothing if not persistent:

> The devil took him to the holy city and had him stand on the highest point of the temple. "If you are the Son of God," he said, "throw yourself down. For it is written:
>
> "'He will command his angels concerning you, and they will lift you up in their hands, so that you will not strike your foot against a stone'" (Matthew 4:5–6).

What a spectacle that would have been, perhaps even making further suffering unnecessary for Jesus. Multitudes would flock to him! Knees would bow! Tongues would confess! All without blood ... albeit without the forgiveness of sins, too (Hebrews 9:22). It must have been attractive, but Jesus replied, "It is also written: 'Do not put the Lord your God to the test'" (Matthew 4:7).

The devil had one more card to play. He paraded before Jesus all the kingdoms of the world and all their splendor. He said, "I will give you all this if you will bow down and worship me." But Jesus, relying again on Scripture to rebut the tempter, said, "Away from me, Satan! For it is written: 'Worship the Lord your God, and serve him only'" (Matthew 4:10).

And the devil left him, the Bible says. Not that Jesus never faced another temptation; but it was a key victory, nonetheless. By it Jesus threw down the gauntlet; he would reverse the curse that resulted from the first Adam's sin. He would accomplish the purpose for which he came: "to destroy the devil's work" (1 John 3:8). As it is written, "Christ redeemed us from the curse of the Law, having become a curse for us—for it is written, 'CURSED IS EVERYONE WHO HANGS ON A TREE'—" (Galatians 3:13, NASB).

FROM THE BIBLE

When the woman saw that the fruit of the tree was good for food and pleasing to the eye, and also desirable for gaining wisdom, she took some and ate it. She also gave some to her husband, who was with her, and he ate it.
—*Genesis 3:6*

I will proclaim the Lord's decree:
  He said to me, "You are my son; today I have become your father.
  Ask me, and I will make the nations your inheritance, the ends of
  the earth your possession.
—*Psalm 2:7–8*

Just as through the disobedience of the one man the many were made sinners, so also through the obedience of the one man the many will be made righteous.
—*Romans 5:19*

For everything in the world—the lust of the flesh, the lust of the eyes, and the pride of life—comes not from the Father but from the world.
—*1 John 2:16*

The reason the Son of God appeared was to destroy the devil's work.
—1 John 3:8

FROM THE HEART

Lord God, thank you that the curse has been lifted. Thank you that sin need not be my master (Romans 6:14). Thank you that I am not under law, but under grace. Thank you that the Son of God appeared to destroy the devil's work, and now I am free to live day by day in the freedom he won. In Jesus' name, amen.

DID YOU KNOW?

Many scholars and Bible teachers see in 1 John 2:16 the summation of the things of this world—"the lust of the flesh, the lust of the eyes, and the pride of life"—as a reflection of the temptation of Eve ("good for food and pleasing to the eye, and also desirable for gaining wisdom") in the temptations of Jesus.

EXPERIENCE THE STORY: FIGHT TEMPTATION WITH SCRIPTURE

In each temptation he faced, Jesus didn't argue with the tempter; he refuted him with the Word of God. Do the same in whatever temptation you face today, quoting Romans 6:14, even aloud if necessary: "Sin shall no longer be [my] master, because [I am] not under the law, but under grace."

GO DEEPER

For further study, read the accounts of Jesus' temptations in Matthew 4:1–11 and Luke 4:1–13.

REFLECTION TIME

Take some time to reflect on these questions, and write down any responses below:

- Do I believe anything so strongly that I would risk my life for it?
- Am I being challenged in some way to stand by my convictions?

They were all downtrodden, unfortunate, and even persecuted.

He was an educated teenager from a noble family in Jerusalem. His city was destroyed and who knows what happened to his family. He was marched off to exile in Babylon. A future derailed. So much potential wasted.

His three friends were taken captive, too. They stayed strong when everyone else wavered. They stood for the truth when everyone else buckled. And what did they get for it? They were arrested, condemned, and thrown into a blazing hot furnace.

An eighty-year-old man prays in private to his God and is betrayed by his coworkers. Thrown to the lions—literally.

A teenage girl has kept herself sexually pure. She's never been touched by a man. And then she's pregnant. No one will believe her story. Her fiancé breaks their engagement.

Even the Son of God, whose Heavenly Father thunders his approval at his baptism, can expect no breaks. He's gone forty days without food. Forty parched days in the wilderness. Forty frigid nights. He's weak. He's famished. He's lonely. Sure enough, that's when the tempter shows up and hits him below the belt.

Maybe you've known similar times. Times when you were downtrodden, unfortunate, and even persecuted. It is only natural at such times to feel like a victim. But from all indications, none of those people did. Though it would have been perfectly understandable in such circumstances, none of those situations produced victims— only victors! Daniel became an influential advisor to the king. His three friends survived the fiery furnace and prompted the king to praise God. Daniel, again, remained faithful to God and endured the lions' den without a scratch. Mary became the mother of the long-awaited Messiah; and Jesus not only endured temptation but triumphed over it.

God's great salvation (Hebrews 2:3) is a salvation from victimhood. He delivers his loved ones from sin, and with it from guilt and shame. The soul who trusts in him is no longer a victim of sin and circumstance, but can be victorious by entrusting their lives into his hands. As Scripture says, "In all ... things we are more than conquerors through him who loved us" (Romans 8:37).

WEEK THREE: SMALL-GROUP STUDY AND DISCUSSION QUESTIONS

Below is a complete list of small-group study and discussion questions for small groups that use this guidebook in conjunction with *The Bible 30-Day Experience DVD Study*. In order to stay within the time limits of your small-group meeting, your small-group leader will choose what questions he or she wants your group to focus on. You will want to bring this guidebook with you to your small group or class.

1. Open in prayer.

2. Go around the room asking everyone to briefly answer this question: "How many presidents, kings, and queens have come and gone in your lifetime?"

3. Introduce video: "Today we study an incident in the life of Daniel, who served numerous kings of Babylon and the Medo-Persian Empire. This video depicts some of those changes."

4. Watch video: "Daniel in the Lions' Den"

5. Question: "Who did you view as the victims in that video?"

6. Question: "Who came across as victorious to you?"

7. Question: "How do you think you would have acted similarly or differently from Daniel's reaction in the lions' den?"

8. Read Daniel 6:1–24.

9. Question: "By the time of the incidents depicted in the video and Scripture reading, Daniel would have been an exile in Babylon for decades. Yet verse 10 says that when he prayed, he opened the windows that faced Jerusalem. What do you think that indicates about Daniel?"

10. Question: "When Daniel learned of the king's order to pray to no one but him for thirty days, verse 10 says, 'He got down on his knees and prayed, giving thanks to his God, just as he had done before.' How else could he have responded to the king's decree?"

11. Question: "Verses 16 and 17 describe Daniel's arrest and imprisonment in the lions' den. Those verses include no

words from Daniel. Do you think that is because:

- Daniel kept silent during his arrest (much like Jesus at his trial)?

- Daniel didn't say anything important?

- Daniel's response was too embarrassing to record?

- Something else?"

12. Question: "Who did Daniel credit for his deliverance in verse 22?"

13. Question: "How does verse 24 counter any suspicion that Daniel's deliverance could have been from natural causes?"

14. Question: "Throughout this incident, was Daniel a victim? a victor? First one, then the other?"

15. Question: "Do you see any parallels between your salvation and Daniel's deliverance? If so, describe them."

16. Question: "Is there any obstacle or threat you face right now? If so, how can you apply Daniel's story to your circumstance?"

17. Any other questions or comments?

18. Close in prayer.

WEEK FOUR THEME:

FROM RELIGION TO RELATIONSHIP

MAIN MESSAGE POINT:

IN PROVIDING SALVATION FROM GUILT AND SHAME, SIN AND DEATH, GOD'S PURPOSE IS NOT THE ESTABLISHMENT OF A RELIGION, BUT THE ENJOYMENT OF A RELATIONSHIP.

THIS WEEK'S MEMORY VERSE:

"IN HIM WE HAVE REDEMPTION THROUGH HIS BLOOD, THE FORGIVENESS OF SINS, IN ACCORDANCE WITH THE RICHES OF GOD'S GRACE."
—EPHESIANS 1:7

OF WHOM THE PROPHETS SPOKE

It was early on the morning of the Sabbath.

Bearded men in long robes passed between rows of pillars as they took their seats in the room, which was lit by a clutter of low-hanging lamps. In the center of the room was an angled desk atop a low platform. Backless benches were arranged on all sides, and looking down on the scene was a balcony filled with the wives and daughters of the men in the room below.

A row of dignified men sat in front of a heavy curtain at the end of the room; one of them rose from his seat and spoke softly to the carpenter, Yeshua ben Yusef—Jesus, the son of Joseph.

Jesus walked to the raised desk in the middle of the synagogue, the same place where as a boy of thirteen he had celebrated his bar mitzvah. All eyes in the room were riveted upon his lean form, made more gaunt by the recent ordeal he had endured during a forty-day fast in the wilderness of Judah. An air of expectation mingled with the smoke from the oil lamps in the room as he ascended the rostrum; sensational rumors had been spreading all over the countryside about the carpenter's son, and he had already taught in other synagogues in the area.

The carpenter's strong voice commenced the first part of the service by reciting a series of prayers and recitations. And then Jesus waited, briefly, while the Chazzan, the man whose duty it was to do so, carried a heavy scroll to the podium. Jesus deftly unrolled the bulky scroll with a skill that betrayed practice while the crowd in the synagogue waited. He found the passage he sought, lifted his eyes to the congregation, and spoke without another look at the scroll.

"The Spirit of the Lord is on me," he said.

Immediately, puzzled looks were exchanged among the men in the rows of seats; this was not the haphtarah, the scheduled reading for the day. This was a jarring departure; he was reading from a passage of his own choosing.

"Because," Jesus continued, the old words ringing with new meaning, "he has anointed me to preach good news to the poor. He has sent me to proclaim freedom for the prisoners and recovery of sight for the blind, to release the oppressed, to proclaim the year of the Lord's favor."

Silence followed his reading. Jesus rolled the scroll together, handed it back to the Chazzan, and sat down in his seat, as a rabbi of that day would do when he was ready to begin teaching. He gazed around the room, meeting the stares of those who watched him.

"Today," he said, "this scripture is fulfilled in your hearing."

With those words, Jesus revealed himself as the One of whom the prophets spoke. It was his mission statement. It was unexpected. Unbelievable to many. And it led the crowd to drive him out of the synagogue and attempt to stone him (Luke 4:14–30).

It would not be the last time. From that moment through the days following his resurrection, Jesus "explained to [his followers] what was said in all the Scriptures concerning himself" (Luke 24:27):

- He was born of a virgin (Isaiah 7:14)
- in Bethlehem (Micah 5:2)
- from the lineage of King David (Isaiah 9:7)
- a messenger would prepare the way for him (Isaiah 40:3–5)
- he would be rejected by his own people (Isaiah 53:3)
- betrayed by a friend (Psalm 41:9)
- crucified with criminals (Isaiah 53:12)
- pierced in his hands, feet, and side (Psalm 22:16, Zechariah 12:10)
- and buried with the rich (Isaiah 53:9)
- he would rise from the dead (Psalm 16:10, 49:15)
- ascend to heaven (Psalm 24:7–10)
- and would be seated at God's right hand (Psalm 68:18, 110:1)

And those are just some of the many Messianic prophecies that were fulfilled in Jesus, all of which were implied in his controversial announcement in Nazareth. All of which he knew, by that time, applied to him. Many of which promised pain and agony. None of which deterred him.

Though he knew the Scriptures that foretold his own suffering and death, he persevered ... all the way to Calvary. He "poured out his life unto death" (Isaiah 53:12) in order to make his life an offering, thus making it possible for you to have an eternal, living relationship with God.

FROM THE BIBLE

And beginning with Moses and all the Prophets, he explained to them what was said in all the Scriptures concerning himself.
—*Luke 24:27*

He did not say anything to them without using a parable. But when he was alone with his own disciples, he explained everything.
—*Mark 4:34*

Philip found Nathanael and told him, "We have found the one Moses wrote about in the Law, and about whom the prophets also wrote—Jesus of Nazareth, the son of Joseph."
—*John 1:45*

"You study the Scriptures diligently because you think that in them you have eternal life. These are the very Scriptures that testify about me."
—*John 5:39*

FROM THE HEART

Jesus, I exalt you as the Anointed One, Messiah, the Christ, the Son of the Living God! You were despised and rejected, for me. You took my pain and bore my suffering. You were pierced for my transgressions and crushed for my iniquities. Your punishment bought my peace and your wounds worked my healing. Thank you for giving me new life by faith, through grace, and making it possible for me to enjoy an eternal, living relationship with you. In Jesus' name, amen.

DID YOU KNOW?

Genesis 3:14–15 is considered to be the first messianic prophecy in the Bible: "So the LORD God said to the serpent, 'Because you have done this … I will put enmity between you and the woman, and between your offspring and hers; he will crush your head, and you will strike his heel.'"

EXPERIENCE THE STORY:
MEDITATE ON A MESSIANIC PROPHECY

Choose one of the twelve messianic prophecies listed in today's reading and look it up in your Bible. Leave your Bible open to that passage so you can see it throughout the day. Every time you see it, pause for a moment to thank God for the fulfillment of that prophecy in Jesus.

GO DEEPER

More than three hundred messianic prophecies were fulfilled by Jesus. Some of them are concentrated in Psalm 22, a psalm written by King David. Read Psalm 22 and note the many allusions to Jesus and his sufferings.

REFLECTION TIME

Answer one or more of the questions below:
- Do I think it was easier or harder for Jesus to persevere, knowing the agonies that were foretold in the Scriptures?
- What does it mean to me that Jesus knew he would suffer but went through with it anyway?
- How does Jesus' fulfillment of so many prophecies affect my faith in him?

THE FULFILLMENT OF THE LAW

Overlooking the Sea of Galilee, near the ruins of the once-thriving towns of Capernaum and Bethsaida, a verdant hillside forms a natural amphitheater. A person can sit atop that hillside and, without amplification, speak to a crowd of hundreds, even thousands. Many people believe it is the site of Jesus' famous "Sermon on the Mount."

The Sermon on the Mount begins with the beatitudes ("Blessed are the poor in spirit, for theirs is the kingdom of heaven," etc.) and includes some of the most famous words ever spoken:

> "You are the salt of the earth" (Matthew 5:13a).
> "You are the light of the world" (Matthew 5:14a).
> "If anyone slaps you on the right cheek, turn to them the other cheek also" (Matthew 5:39b).
> "Where your treasure is, there your heart will be also" (Matthew 6:21).
> "No one can serve two masters" (Matthew 6:24a).
> "Do not judge, or you too will be judged" (Matthew 7:1).
> "Ask and it will be given to you; seek and you will find; knock and the door will be opened to you" (Matthew 7:7).

In these words and more, Jesus gave his followers his *mishnah*, the collection and distillation of a rabbi's teachings for his students to memorize and follow. In issuing this sermon, Jesus was doing what many rabbis of his day did. But he was doing far, far more.

When Jesus "went up on a mountainside and sat down ... and ... began to teach" (Matthew 5:1–2), he was doing something very purposeful and symbolic. His actions and his words evoked another man and another mountain. His Jewish audience would not have missed the significance, especially after Jesus began to speak.

Hundreds of years before, after God's people had been delivered from slavery in Egypt, they camped at the foot of a mountain: Mount Sinai. They waited while Moses, the instrument God used in their deliverance, went up onto the mountain. When he returned after forty days and forty nights in the presence of God, he carried tablets of stone bearing the commandments of God. From that day forward, nothing was more important to the people of Israel than the Law of Moses.

Centuries later, God spoke through the prophet Jeremiah and announced:

> "The days are coming," declares the LORD, "when I will make a new covenant with the people of Israel and with the people of Judah.
> It will not be like the covenant I made with their ancestors when I took them by the hand to lead them out of Egypt, because they broke my covenant, though I was a husband to them," declares the LORD.
> "This is the covenant I will make with the people of Israel after that time," declares the LORD.
> "I will put my law in their minds and write it on their hearts. I will be their God, and they will be my people." ...
> "For I will forgive their wickedness and will remember their sins no more" (Jeremiah 31:31–34).

When Jesus sat on that Galilean hillside and said, "'Do not think that I have come to abolish the Law or the Prophets; I have not come to abolish them but to fulfill them'" (Matthew 5:17), his listeners would surely have understood that a New Moses—the very fulfillment of Jeremiah's promise—spoke to them. Moses heard God's voice and received the Law on the Mountain of God; Jesus, the very Word of God himself, presented himself as the fulfillment of the Law on the Mount of the Beatitudes.

With an authority beyond what any human could claim, Jesus told the crowds, "You have heard it said (that is, by Moses, in the Law) … but I say to you." Over and over again, he spoke of the Law of Moses and then amplified it, intensified it, adding, "Be perfect, therefore, as your heavenly Father is perfect" (Matthew 5:48).

Far from negating or abolishing the Law, Jesus took it further and deeper, to a standard of holiness that would have been impossible … unless the day Jeremiah promised had come. It was a new covenant, a covenant written in the blood of Jesus and made possible by his work on the cross. Through him—and the indwelling presence of the Holy Spirit—the Law would be written on people's minds and hearts.

FROM THE BIBLE

"Do not think that I have come to abolish the Law or the Prophets; I have not come to abolish them but to fulfill them."
—*Matthew 5:17*

This righteousness is given through faith in Jesus Christ to all who believe.
—*Romans 3:22*

For this reason Christ is the mediator of a new covenant, that those who are called may receive the promised eternal inheritance—now that he has died as a ransom to set them free from the sins committed under the first covenant.
—*Hebrews 9:15*

But you have come to Mount Zion, to the city of the living God, the heavenly Jerusalem. You have come to thousands upon thousands of angels in joyful assembly, to the church of the firstborn, whose names are written in heaven. You have come to God, the Judge of all, to the spirits of the righteous made perfect, to Jesus the mediator of a new covenant. …
—*Hebrews 12:22–24a*

FROM THE HEART

Lord God Almighty, thank You for writing your Word on my heart, that I might not sin against you (Psalm 119:11). Thank you that in Christ you have fulfilled the Law and the promise of Jeremiah in me.

You have forgiven my sins and remember them no more. Thank you for helping me to live day by day, by the power of Your Holy Spirit who lives in me, in a way befitting someone whose name is written in heaven. In Jesus' name, amen.

EXPERIENCE THE STORY: THE GOLDEN RULE

In his Sermon on the Mount, Jesus said, "So in everything, do to others what you would have them do to you, for this sums up the Law and the Prophets" (Matthew 7:12). Make a conscious effort today to follow this "golden rule" in all you do.

GO DEEPER

For further study, read the full Sermon on the Mount in Matthew, chapters 5–7.

REFLECTION TIME

Take some time to reflect on these questions below:

- What does it mean to me that I "have come to Mount Zion, to the city of the living God, the heavenly Jerusalem"?
- Does my life reflect the joy of someone who has "come to thousands upon thousands of angels in joyful assembly, to the church of the firstborn, whose names are written in heaven"?
- What does it mean that I have "come to God, the Judge of all, to the spirits of the righteous made perfect, to Jesus the mediator of a new covenant"? How can I better live in that truth in my daily life?

BREAD OF HEAVEN

The crowd just kept growing.

Jesus and his closest followers had crossed to the far side of the lake, but hordes of people caught up with them and gathered to hear Jesus teach.

Jesus sat down, as if to teach, and beckoned to Philip, one of the Twelve. "Where will we buy enough bread for this crowd?" he asked.

Philip shook his head. "Buy bread? For this crowd?" The crowd already numbered more than five thousand, counting only the men! "That would take half a year's wages!"

Another who had been standing nearby said, "Send them away, Lord. Let them go into town to buy food."

Jesus shook his head. "Why don't you give them something to eat?"

Philip and the other disciple began to protest, but Andrew shuffled closer, herding a young boy in front of him. "This boy has five little loaves and a couple of fish," he said. "But how far will that go?"

Jesus nodded. He smiled at the boy and then looked up at his followers. "Have the people sit down."

As they set to work, Jesus invited the boy to sit down beside him. They talked like old friends, and when the crowd was seated on the grassy hillside, Jesus stood. He lifted the two small circles of flatbread toward the sky and spoke a blessing.

He paused, as if listening. Then he broke each of the loaves and handed portions to his followers to distribute to the crowd. Soon he started handing pieces of fish to them, and those were likewise given out.

When Jesus' followers reported that everyone had eaten, he nodded. "Gather all that remains. Let nothing be wasted."

A few moments later, twelve baskets of bread were set at Jesus' feet by his disciples. Soon the realization of what Jesus had done began to ripple through the crowd. There was a buzz of excitement. Many said, "Surely this is the Prophet who is to come into the world."

The feeding of the five thousand was a miracle. Obviously. But what is not so obvious to us as we read about it twenty centuries later is the weighty symbolism of the miracle.

Remember, everyone present on that Galilean hillside was a Jew. They had all been raised on the rich history of their people, which included the Exodus, the forty years of wandering in the wilderness—and God's provision of manna, when the Lord had responded to the hungry multitude by saying, "I will rain down bread from heaven for you" (Exodus 16:4a).

In feeding the five thousand, Jesus was not just meeting the need of a moment; he was identifying himself as the one who sent manna in the wilderness.

But why have the disciples collect the leftovers? Why did Jesus apparently make a point of an abundance being left over? That, too, held significance that the watching crowd would surely have grasped; it echoed an incident in the ministry of Elisha:

> A man came from Baal Shalishah, bringing the man of God twenty loaves of barley bread baked from the first ripe grain, along with some heads of new grain. "Give it to the people to eat," Elisha said.
>
> "How can I set this before a hundred men?" his servant asked.
>
> But Elisha answered, "Give it to the people to eat. For this is what the LORD says: 'They will eat and have some left over.'" Then he set it before them, and they ate and had some left over, according to the word of the LORD (2 Kings 4:42–44).

A hungry crowd. A miraculous provision. And some left over. But even that doesn't capture the full extent of Jesus' words and actions on that day. In feeding the five thousand, he was not only presenting himself as the One who sends bread ... he was declaring himself to be the Bread of Life: "'I am the bread of life. Whoever comes to me will never go hungry ..." (John 6:35a).

The people on that Galilean hillside were filled with wonder. But Jesus wanted more than that for them. He wanted them to be filled, not with the bread he multiplied, but with himself, the Bread of Life. And his desire is the same today. He does not just give bread to the hungry; he gives himself to all who ask—a miraculous and abundant provision.

FROM THE BIBLE

Then the LORD said to Moses, "I will rain down bread from heaven for you. ...

In the morning there was a layer of dew around the camp. When the dew was gone, thin flakes like frost on the ground appeared on the desert floor. When the Israelites saw it, they said to each other, "What is it?" For they did not know what it was.

Moses said to them, "It is the bread the LORD has given you to eat."
—*Exodus 16:4a, 13b–15*

"I am the bread of life. Your ancestors ate the manna in the wilderness, yet they died. But here is the bread that comes down from heaven, which anyone may eat and not die. I am the living bread that came down from heaven. Whoever eats this bread will live forever. This bread is my flesh, which I will give for the life of the world."
—*John 6:48–51*

"Just as the living Father sent me and I live because of the Father, so the one who feeds on me will live because of me. This is the bread that came down from heaven. Your ancestors ate manna and died, but whoever feeds on this bread will live forever."
—*John 6:57–58*

FROM THE HEART

Lord Jesus, you are the Bread of Life. Live in me. Be my daily bread. Be my manna, my provision, my life, and health. Help me, Lord, not to "snack" at your table, but to feast on you, to eat my fill of your presence and power. And let my life overflow and result in blessings on those around me. In Jesus' name, amen.

DID YOU KNOW?
The feeding of the five thousand is the only miracle of Jesus that is reported in all four Gospels—Matthew, Mark, Luke, and John.

EXPERIENCE THE STORY:
BREAK BREAD
Make it a point today to include bread in at least one meal. As you say grace (alone or with others), break the bread with a prayer for Jesus, the Bread of Life, thanking Him for sustaining you and being with you throughout the day.

GO DEEPER
For further study, read John's account of the feeding of the five thousand in John 6:1–15 and then read Jesus' discourse on the Bread of Life in John 6:25–59.

REFLECTION TIME
Reflect on one or more of these questions, and write your responses below:
- In what ways is Jesus the "Bread of Life" to me?
- How can I work, not for food that spoils, but for food that endures to eternal life, which the Son of Man will give me?

THE RESURRECTION AND THE LIFE

We know it happened at least three times. There may have been others that weren't recorded (John 21:25).

One day a prominent citizen named Jairus dropped to his knees in front of Jesus. "My daughter has just died," the man said. "Come and put your hand on her, and she will live." When Jesus entered the man's house, he took the girl by the hand and told her to get up. Life returned to her body, and she arose as if she had just been napping.

Another time, Jesus went to a town called Nain. As he approached the town, a large funeral procession appeared. A young man—the only son of his widowed mother—was being carried out to burial. Jesus halted the procession and touched the young man's funeral bier. He spoke to the corpse: "Young man, arise!" The widow's son sat up, said something, and Jesus returned the boy to his mother.

Still another time, a message was sent to Jesus from his friends Mary and Martha that their brother, Lazarus, was sick. Obviously, they wanted Jesus to come and heal him. But instead, he delayed. When he and his followers arrived at the home of Lazarus, he had already died. And been buried. So Jesus went to the tomb, a cave with a stone laid across the entrance. "Take away the stone," he said. Martha thought he needed to be reminded: "He has been in the tomb for four days; the smell will be terrible." But Jesus insisted, and the stone was rolled away from the entrance. Then he called out: "Lazarus, come out!" And Mary and Martha's brother stumbled to the entrance of the tomb, still bound tightly in the linen burial clothes. The scene froze for a moment, until Jesus said, "Someone take off the grave clothes and let him go!"

Three resurrections. Each one a great miracle, of course. But each one was also a sign.

Centuries before, the prophet Elijah was staying in the home of a widow in Zarephath. Her son became ill and died. But Elijah pried the boy from her arms, carried him upstairs, and laid him on the bed. Three times the prophet stretched himself out on the corpse and prayed for God to restore the boy's life. Moments later, Elijah carried him back downstairs and returned him, alive, to his mother.

Elijah's successor, Elisha, was also provided an upstairs room by a woman in Shunem. That woman's son became suddenly ill and died in his mother's arms. Perhaps thinking of Elijah and the widow of Zarephath, she carried her son's corpse upstairs and laid him on the bed in the room she kept for the prophet. Then she went to Elisha and told him that her son had died. He returned with her, went into his room, shut the door, and prayed. As Elijah had done, Elisha stretched himself out on the corpse. The boy's body warmed, but he didn't awaken. So Elijah got up, paced, and then stretched out on the boy again. This time, the boy sneezed seven times and opened his eyes. Elisha summoned the Shunammite woman and said, "Take your son."

Every mourner at the house of Jairus knew about the widow's son and the Shunammite woman's son, as did every mourner in the funeral procession at Nain and at the tomb of Lazarus. None of them could miss the significance of what Jesus did on those three occasions when he raised the dead. And none of them could miss the differences, either.

Elijah and Elisha both stretched themselves out on the body of the deceased. Jesus merely touched Jairus's daughter's hand. In the case of the widow's son at Nain, he touched the funeral bier. And at the raising of Lazarus, he merely spoke.

Elijah stretched out three times on the boy's form as he prayed. Elisha did so twice. When Jesus raised the dead, there was no delay, no uncertainty. He spoke: "Get up," "Arise," "Come forth!" And the dead lived.

The most important difference, however, lay in one other thing. Elijah and Elisha were able to raise the dead by praying to God; Jesus revealed himself as far more than a prophet or a man of God. He proclaimed to Mary, "I am the resurrection and the life" (John

11:25). Not "I restore life," but "I am life." He is resurrection. He is life. And his life is imparted to all who by faith enter into a loving, living relationship with him.

FROM THE BIBLE

The blind receive sight, the lame walk, those who have leprosy are cleansed, the deaf hear, the dead are raised, and the good news is proclaimed to the poor.
—*Luke 7:22*

Jesus said to her, "I am the resurrection and the life. The one who believes in me will live, even though they die; and whoever lives by believing in me will never die."
—*John 11:25–26*

In him was life, and that life was the light of all mankind.
—*John 1:4*

For as the Father has life in himself, so he has granted the Son also to have life in himself.
—*John 5:26*

I have been crucified with Christ and I no longer live, but Christ lives in me. The life I now live in the body, I live by faith in the Son of God, who loved me and gave himself for me.
—*Galatians 2:20*

When Christ, who is your life, appears, then you also will appear with him in glory.
—*Colossians 3:4*

FROM THE HEART

Lord, you revealed yourself as the Resurrection and the Life to Jairus by raising his daughter from the dead. You revealed yourself as the Resurrection and the Life by raising the widow of Nain's son. You revealed yourself as the Resurrection and the Life by calling Lazarus out of the tomb. And you have done so also by imparting life to me, by grace, through faith, so that I no longer live, but you live in me. Thank you for helping me day by day to live by faith in the Son of God, who loved me and gave himself for me. In Jesus' name, amen.

DID YOU KNOW?

The village of Nain, where Jesus raised the widow's son from the dead, was located on the same hill as Shunem, where Elisha raised the Shunammite's son. The two towns are approximately two miles from each other.

EXPERIENCE THE STORY: THE LIGHT OF LIFE

Keep a light (or candle) burning where you can see it throughout the day to remind you of John 1:4: "In him was life, and that life was the light of all mankind." Pause briefly whenever you notice it and give thanks for the life of Christ in you.

GO DEEPER

For further study, read the accounts of the three resurrections Jesus performed (besides his own) in Mark 5:21–43, Luke 7:11–17, and John 11:1–44.

REFLECTION TIME

Take some time to reflect on these questions below:
- Who do I identify most with in the stories of Elijah, Elisha, and Jesus? With the prophets? The dead children? The grieving parents? The onlookers? Why?
- In what area of my life do I need Jesus' life-giving power?
- What does it mean, practically, for me to live by faith in the Son of God, who loved me and gave himself for me?

THE REBEL KING

As Jesus and the others joined the river of pilgrims flowing toward the Holy City, some in the crowd recognized him. Excitement pulsed through the crowd as more and more of the pilgrims flocked to him. *Jesus of Nazareth. The miracle worker! They say he raised Lazarus of Bethany from the dead!* And …

And …

He was riding on a donkey.

Murmurs of amazement turned to shouts of exhilaration. Word spread up and down the dusty path, and soon people were running toward Jesus, while others lined the road toward the city. Some could hardly believe their eyes. Others wept.

No one knew who started it, but someone in the crowd spread a piece of clothing on the path ahead of the donkey Jesus rode. Another followed suit, and then another. Soon, children and women ran to nearby trees, tore off the branches, and laid them on the road, too. The crowd began to press closer and closer to him on every side. Laughter and song filled the air. Then someone shouted: "Hosanna," a word that meant "save us!" Others soon joined the chorus, until the cries echoed off the gleaming walls of the city:

"Hosanna to the Son of David!"
"Blessed is he who comes in the name of the Lord!"
"Hosanna in the highest heaven!" (Matthew 21:9b).

By the time Jesus entered Jerusalem that day, his entourage had swelled from a mere dozen to thousands, all of whom wanted to see him and hear his words. The crowd followed him all the way to the Temple, where he dismounted. Then, as crowds still trailed him with cries of "Hosanna" on their lips:

> Jesus entered the temple courts and drove out all who were buying and selling there. He overturned the tables of the moneychangers and the benches of those selling doves. "It is written," he said to them, "'My house will be called a house of prayer,' but you are making it 'a den of robbers'" (Matthew 21:12–13).

That first "Palm Sunday" electrified the crowds of pilgrims entering the city for the upcoming celebration of Passover. They recognized in Jesus' entry into Jerusalem the fulfillment of the prophet Zechariah's words:

> Rejoice greatly, Daughter Zion!
>   Shout, Daughter Jerusalem!
> See, your king comes to you, righteous and victorious, lowly and riding on a donkey, on a colt, the foal of a donkey (Zechariah 9:9).

They also saw in Jesus' appearance that day the fulfillment of the prophet Malachi's promise:

> "Then suddenly the Lord you are seeking will come to his temple; the messenger of the covenant, whom you desire, will come," says the LORD Almighty (Malachi 3:1b).

They also saw something more—something that many Bible readers today miss.

A couple centuries before, a ruler named Antiochus occupied the holy city of Jerusalem. He killed and carried thousands into captivity, and plundered the Temple. He placed an idol in the Temple, and forced the people to sacrifice pigs, which Jews considered unclean, or face severe punishment. Many were tortured or scourged or crucified. But a man named Judas Maccabeus ("Judas the Hammer") and his brothers led a rebellion. They defeated Antiochus's armies and drove them out of the land. Judas Maccabeus and his brothers entered the holy city "singing hymns of praise and thanks-giving, while carrying palm branches and playing harps, cymbals, and lyres" (1 Maccabees 13:51, GNT). And Judas the Hammer im-mediately cleansed the Temple, destroyed Antiochus's idol, and re-stored the worship of God to its proper place. For years to come, the coins of that era would be stamped with palm branches, the family emblem of the Maccabees.

So, when Jesus entered the city that day, on a donkey, to cries of "Hosanna" and waving palm branches, and cleansed the Temple of the merchants and moneychangers, all who saw him would have gotten the message: He was the long-awaited deliverer, the rebel king who would save his people.

They didn't understand, however, that the kingdom Jesus estab-lished was not political or temporal:

> Pilate ... summoned Jesus and asked him, "Are you the king of the Jews?" ...
> Jesus said, "My kingdom is not of this world. If it were, my servants would fight to prevent my arrest by the Jewish leaders. But now my kingdom is from another place" (John 18:33, 36).

Our rebel king, Jesus, established a kingdom that is not of this world, but no less real. It is a spiritual, eternal, and relational real-ity. A reality of the heart. A kingdom of the spirit.

FROM THE BIBLE

"The days are coming," declares the LORD, "when I will raise up for David a righteous Branch, a King who will reign wisely and do what is just and right in the land.

In his days Judah will be saved and Israel will live in safety.

This is the name by which he will be called:

The LORD Our Righteous Savior.

—*Jeremiah 23:5–6*

"The kingdom of God is within you."

—*Luke 17:21 (NIV, 1984)*

FROM THE HEART

Lord Jesus, you taught your followers to pray for your kingdom to come; I pray it now. Let your kingdom come, let your will be done in my heart and life as promptly and fully as it is in heaven.

DID YOU KNOW?

The Jewish holiday of Hanukkah, also called the Festival of Lights, celebrates the rededication of the Temple in Jerusalem during the Maccabean period. After the forces of Antiochus had been driven from the Temple, the Maccabees discovered that all but one day's supply of the ritual olive oil used for the lamp in the Temple had been profaned. Miraculously, the supply lasted eight days—the time it took for new oil to be produced. To this day, the Festival of Lights lasts eight days, until all eight branches of the menorah are alight.

EXPERIENCE THE STORY: RETURN SOMETHING BORROWED

The Gospel writers tell us that Jesus rode into Jerusalem that first Palm Sunday on a borrowed donkey, but they don't tell us how or when the donkey was returned to its owner. There may be something in your possession that hasn't been returned yet to its owner. If so, make a point today to return it as a simple and easy reminder of the integrity of Jesus.

GO DEEPER

For further study, compare the accounts of Jesus' triumphal entry into Jerusalem the Sunday before his crucifixion in Matthew 21:1–11, Mark 11:1–17, Luke 19:28–48, and John 12:12–18.

REFLECTION TIME

Reflect on one or more of these questions below:
- What effect has Jesus' kingship had on my life?
- Does Jesus' kingship produce any practical results in how I live my life?
- What areas of my life need to be submitted to the kingly rule of Jesus?

BREAD AND CUP

Imagine yourself as one of Jesus' twelve closest followers and friends in the upper room. The impending start of the Passover Feast has Jerusalem bursting with pilgrims and bristling with tension. The group around the low table is no exception. Everyone seems a bit out of sorts. On edge. Uneasy. When the conversation around the table lags, Jesus speaks.

"I have been looking forward to eating this Passover with you before I suffer," he says.

There it is. Again. These last few days Jesus has frequently referred to suffering, even death. It is beginning to bother you—and apparently the others as well. A shadow seems to cloud every face.

Jesus speaks of many things during the meal that follows, the centerpiece of which is the deliciously aromatic Passover Lamb, unleavened bread, and bitter herbs that remind you of the first Passover, when God delivered his people from slavery in Egypt. He even speaks of someone in the group betraying him, and in the confused chatter that follows, Judas arises and leaves—maybe to make arrangements for the festival or give something to the poor.

Then, after pronouncing the *Birka Hamazon*, "The Blessing After the Meal," Jesus picks up a piece of bread and breaks it, repeatedly, meaningfully. He gives a piece to each one around the table, saying, "This is my body, given for you." Then he lifts the symbolic third cup of wine at the meal, the cup of redemption, which has always symbolized the blood of the Pascal lamb. But he departs again from the *haggada*, the usual script. Instead, he says, "This cup is the new covenant in my blood, which is poured out for you."

At that point in the meal, a cup of wine is usually poured by the host in honor of Elijah. But Jesus skips that for some reason. He nods to the disciple closest to the door, who opens the door on cue, signaling the final *hallel*, the closing hymn of the celebration, which concludes:

> The stone the builders rejected has become the cornerstone;
>   the LORD has done this, and it is marvelous in our eyes.
> The LORD has done it this very day;
>   let us rejoice today and be glad.
> LORD, save us!
>   LORD, grant us success!
> Blessed is he who comes in the name of the LORD.
>   From the house of the LORD we bless you.
> The LORD is God, and he has made his light shine on us.
> With boughs in hand, join in the festal procession up to the
>   horns of the altar.
> You are my God, and I will praise you; you are my God, and I
>   will exalt you.
> Give thanks to the LORD, for he is good; his love endures for
>   ever (Psalm 118:22–29).

At the time, of course, neither you nor any of your companions understand the significance of what just happened. But over the next few days and weeks, as Jesus is arrested and tried, tortured and crucified—and then raised from the dead and ascended into the heavens, its impact hits you.

That meal in the upper room began as the traditional *Seder*, the symbolic meal to celebrate the deliverance of Israel from slavery in Egypt. But Jesus turned it into something else that night. He subtracted nothing from the historic symbolism of lamb and herb, bread and wine. But he amplified it, opening his follower's eyes to the deeper, greater significance that had always been there, waiting for fulfillment in the light of Jesus' Passion.

The events of Jesus' Passion revealed so much. There was the lamb at the center of the feast, which represented Jesus himself, the Lamb of God who takes away the sins of the world. There was the three-layered *matza*, or unleavened bread, from which the middle layer was removed, broken, wrapped, buried ... and brought back.

But the most significant elements of the meal to Jesus were the bread that—broken—represented his body, which was soon to be beaten, pierced, and nailed to a cross. And "the cup of redemption," representing his blood, which would be poured out for the redemption of the world. In that meal, on that night, Jesus explained his redemptive and relational promise: "Whoever eats my flesh and drinks my blood has eternal life, and I will raise them up at the last day. For my flesh is real food and my blood is real drink. Whoever eats my flesh and drinks my blood remains in me, and I in them" (John 6:54–56).

FROM THE BIBLE

On the first day of the Festival of Unleavened Bread, when it was customary to sacrifice the Passover lamb, ... while they were eating, Jesus took bread, and when he had given thanks, he broke it and gave it to his disciples, saying, "Take it; this is my body." Then he took a cup, and when he had given thanks, he gave it to them, and they all drank from it. "This is my blood of the covenant, which is poured out for many," he said to them. "Truly I tell you, I will not drink again from the fruit of the vine until that day when I drink it new in the kingdom of God." When they had sung a hymn, they went out to the Mount of Olives.
—*Mark 14:12a, 22–26*

FROM THE HEART

Lord Jesus, you are my life and my portion. You are Living Bread and the Cup of Redemption to me. You are the stone the builders rejected that has become the cornerstone. Thank you for your salvation! You have made your light shine on me. You are my God, and I will praise you; you are my God, and I will exalt you. In Jesus' name, amen.

DID YOU KNOW?

The Passover meal includes something called the *afikomen*, a word that translates to "that which comes later." It is the middle layer of a three-layered matza, unleavened bread that is kept in a special pouch. During the meal, the host removes the middle layer of the matza from the pouch. He breaks it and sets half aside; he then wraps the remaining half—the *afikomen*—in a white linen cloth and hides it away somewhere nearby. Later, any children who are at the meal search for the *afikomen*; when they find it, the host removes it from the linen shroud and shares it with the participants. It is the last solid substance to be consumed at the meal and its taste is intended to be the last, lingering taste of the celebration—to stay with the participants when they leave the table.

EXPERIENCE THE STORY: THE *AFIKOMEN*

The next time you celebrate communion, pause for a moment before taking the bread and the cup to remember the afikomen, the middle layer of the three-layer matza which is removed, broken, wrapped, buried, brought back; ... and say a prayer thanking Jesus for His abiding presence with you always.

GO DEEPER

For further study, consider researching and locating a ministry or church that presents a Passover Seder meal in the context of Jesus' teaching. It can be a rewarding discovery.

REFLECTION TIME

Take some time to reflect on these questions below:
- If I picture myself as one of the disciples around the table at the last supper, with whom do I identify most? Peter? John? Judas? Someone else? And why?
- Is Jesus' life in me as real to me as physical food and drink? If not, why not?
- How can I experience the "taste" of Jesus' presence with me throughout this day?

The assumption was that the Messiah would conform to the religious conventions of first-century Judaism.

In other words, everyone expected that the Messiah would be Jewish, of course. He would be religious. He would keep all the laws of Moses. He would fastidiously observe the Sabbath. He would worship at the Temple. He would keep the feasts. He would reward the right people and punish the wrong people. He would lead Israel to victory and defeat—humiliate, even—the Romans.

Then came Jesus, the rabbi from Nazareth, who seemed to fulfill prophecies—just the wrong ones. He claimed to be the "fulfillment" of the Law. He seemed to talk about destroying the Temple. He associated with all the wrong people, and repeatedly antagonized the most upstanding religious people of his day. To top it all off, rather than standing up to the Romans and establishing a new, politically triumphant, Israel ... he ended up dying on a Roman cross.

But from Jesus' perspective, it was all according to plan. He turned the religious conventions on their heads because he had not come to spread religion. He had not come to exalt or abolish the Law of Moses—he was its fulfillment. The tears he shed were not for the Temple, but for the lost sheep of Israel who could not recognize that one greater than the Temple had come to them. His mission was not to conquer a country but to conquer the human heart. His purpose was not to establish a religion but to initiate and propagate a relationship, through which all humanity could enjoy forgiveness (because Jesus is our high priest, and when He enters a life, He brings full atonement), righteousness (because Jesus is the fulfillment of the law, and when He enters a life, He brings His righteousness), and power (because Jesus is king, and when He enters a life, He brings the power of His presence and rule).

As you prepare for the final week of *The Bible 30-Day Experience*, take time to focus your attention and action on your relationship with God through Jesus Christ. Like any relationship, it will grow and you will appreciate it more as you invest more time and attention to it. In this relationship, the depth and power of His love for you is infinitely more important than the perfection of your performance. As you prepare for worship, remember to "draw near to God with a sincere heart and with the full assurance that faith brings" (Hebrews 10:22).

WEEK FOUR: SMALL-GROUP STUDY AND DISCUSSION QUESTIONS

Below is a complete list of small-group study and discussion questions for small groups that use this guidebook in conjunction with *The Bible 30-Day Experience DVD Study*. In order to stay within the time limits of your small-group meeting, your small-group leader will choose what questions he or she wants your group to focus on. You will want to bring this guidebook with you to your small group or class.

1. Open in prayer.

2. Go around the room asking everyone to briefly answer this question: "Have you ever rescued someone? Has someone ever rescued you?"

3. Watch video: "One Dark Night"

4. Question: "As you watched that video, what sorts of things were you thinking and feeling?"

5. Question: "Did you identify with one person in the video more than another? If so, who? And why?"

6. Introduce Scripture reading: "The Scripture passage we are going to study, from the Gospel of John, is part of the Upper Room conversation Jesus had with his disciples on the night of his last supper."

7. Read John 15:1–17.

8. Question: "Would you describe Jesus' words in this passage as 'relational' or 'religious'? And why?"

9. Question: "Jesus talks repeatedly about his followers 're-maining' (KJV: 'abiding') in him. What do you think he means by that?"

10. Question: "As Jesus spoke these words, he knew that his arrest, trial, and crucifixion were imminent. How do you think that knowledge affected what he said to his followers?"

11. Question: "What did Jesus mean by saying, 'apart from me you can do nothing' (v. 5)?"

12. Question: "How, in practical terms, do you think we are supposed to 'remain in' Jesus?"

13. Question: "Do Jesus' words here make him sound like he's establishing a religion? If so, how? If not, why not?"

14. Question: "Are you 'remaining' or 'abiding' in Jesus, like he says in these verses? If so, how? If not, why not?"

15. Question: "Are you 'bearing fruit,' like Jesus says in these verses? If so, how? If not, why not?"

16. Question: "Are you loving your fellow disciples, like Jesus tells his followers to do in these verses? If so, how? If not, why not?"

17. Any other questions or comments?

18. Close in prayer.

WEEK FIVE THEME:

FROM DARKNESS TO LIGHT

MAIN MESSAGE POINT:

GOD HAS DELIVERED US FROM THE DARKNESS OF CONFUSION, FEAR, AND DOUBT, AND HAS BESTOWED ON US THE LIGHT OF A NEW PURPOSE, PEACE, AND PRESENCE.

THIS WEEK'S MEMORY VERSE:

"FOR YOU WERE ONCE DARKNESS, BUT NOW YOU ARE LIGHT IN THE LORD. LIVE AS CHILDREN OF LIGHT."
—EPHESIANS 5:8

THE LIVING TEMPLE

They were the words that got him killed.

They were recorded in John's Gospel. In the other Gospels they are only referred to as the grounds for a charge of blasphemy at Jesus' trial before the Sanhedrin: "Destroy this temple, and I will raise it again in three days."

According to John, Jesus said it on the same occasion when he entered the Temple courts and drove out the moneychangers and hawkers of cattle, sheep, and doves, saying, "Get these out of here! Stop turning my Father's house into a market!" (John 2:16).

> The Jews then responded to him, "What sign can you show us to prove your authority to do all this?"
>
> Jesus answered them, "Destroy this temple, and I will raise it again in three days."
>
> They replied, "It has taken forty-six years to build this temple, and you are going to raise it in three days?" But the temple he had spoken of was his body (John 2:18–21).

At the time, neither Jesus' closest followers and friends nor his most strident enemies understood. His followers were more or less dumbfounded (John 2:22); his enemies thought he was talking about the physical Temple, the shining summit of Herod the Great's building projects, which had been "under construction" since before Jesus had been born.

But Jesus wasn't talking about the Jerusalem Temple, of course. He was uttering a prophecy of his own resurrection. He was telling them, "Kill me, and I'll rise again."

So why didn't he just say that? Why did he have to go and confuse everyone with his talk of a "temple?"

It wasn't confusion. It was fulfillment.

The temple in Jerusalem was considered the dwelling place of God on earth (Psalm 84:1). It was the place of his presence, "the place where [his] glory dwells" (Psalm 26:8). The prophet Ezekiel promised that there would come a day when God would establish a new kind of temple:

> My dwelling place will be with them; I will be their God, and they will be my people. Then the nations will know that I the LORD make Israel holy, when my sanctuary is among them forever (Ezekiel 37:27–28).

One day Jesus and his disciples were hiking through fields of ripe grain on the Sabbath. They had worked up an appetite by this time, so several of them plucked the heads from the stalks and ate. Some Pharisees had been watching and confronted Jesus.

"Look!" one of them said. "Your disciples are breaking the Sabbath by harvesting those heads of grain!"

Jesus said to them. "Have you not read what David did when he and his companions were hungry?" David, of course, was the highly revered king of Israel, the model for the Messiah. "They entered the house of God and ate the consecrated bread—which was unlawful for anyone but a priest to eat. Of course, maybe you haven't read in the Law that the priests in the temple work on the Sabbath and yet aren't blamed for it. So let me just tell you this: something greater than the temple is here."

Something greater than the Temple.

Jesus had used phrases like that before. He had referred to someone greater than Jonah and greater than Solomon, by which he meant himself.

So, when he says, "Something greater than the Temple is here" (Matthew 12:6), he is referring to himself. In other words, Jesus not only identified himself as a temple, he proclaimed himself as greater than the Jerusalem Temple.

Jesus is the living Temple, the actual presence of God. John wrote, "The Word became flesh and made his dwelling among us. We have seen his glory, the glory of the one and only Son, who came from the

Father, full of grace and truth" (John 1:14).

Jesus is the fulfillment of everything the Jerusalem Temple pointed to. He is the presence of God. He is the Holy of Holies. He is "the place where [his] glory dwells" (Psalm 26:8). And, because of his death, resurrection, ascension, and the sending of his Holy Spirit to the church, he dwells in every believer. The Temple is no longer outside you; he is within you. The light of his glory, symbolized by the golden lamp stand in the ancient temple, now brightens the heart of every believer, "For God ... made his light shine in our hearts to give us the light of the knowledge of God's glory displayed in the face of Christ" (2 Corinthians 4:6).

FROM THE BIBLE

"Then have them make a sanctuary for me, and I will dwell among them."
—*Exodus 25:8*

"I tell you that something greater than the temple is here."
—*Matthew 12:6*

Jesus replied, "Anyone who loves me will obey my teaching. My Father will love them, and we will come to them and make our home with them."
—*John 14:23*

And I heard a loud voice from the throne saying, "Look! God's dwelling place is now among the people, and he will dwell with them. They will be his people, and God himself will be with them and be their God."
—*Revelation 21:3*

FROM THE HEART

Lord Jesus, dwell in me. Fill me with the light of your presence and glory; let your peace and power reign in my heart and life. Fill me with your grace and truth. Amen.

DID YOU KNOW?

The Jerusalem Temple was destroyed a few decades after Jesus' death, burial, and resurrection. A rebellion against Rome that started in 66 AD resulted in the destruction of the Temple by the Roman general (later emperor) Titus in 70 AD. This fulfilled Jesus' prediction in Mark 13:2: "Not one stone here will be left on another; every one will be thrown down."

EXPERIENCE THE STORY: CLEANSE THE TEMPLE

The Bible says, "Do you not know that your bodies are temples of the Holy Spirit, who is in you, whom you have received from God? You are not your own" (1 Corinthians 6:19). As you bathe today, remember Jesus cleansing the Jerusalem Temple and thank Him for the sanctifying work of the Holy Spirit in your life.

GO DEEPER

For further study, read carefully Hebrews 7–10, in which Jesus' superiority over the Temple system of priests and sacrifices is outlined.

REFLECTION TIME

Reflect on one or more of these questions, and record your responses below:

- Are there areas in my life that do not reflect "the light of the knowledge of God's glory" (2 Corinthians 4:6)?
- How can the grace of Jesus change that in my life?

THE ULTIMATE SACRIFICE

It would not be the last time God saved by counter-intuitive means.

The people of Israel had traveled long and hard since their deliverance from slavery. They had received God's Law. They had survived on manna and quail. They had constructed a tabernacle. And, through it all, they had complained.

God had warned them repeatedly, through Moses. And still they grumbled and groused. Finally, God sent poisonous snakes into the camp, and they wreaked havoc among the people. Many were bitten; many died.

The people recognized the snakes as God's judgment, and some of them went to Moses and asked him to pray for God to get rid of the snakes.

So Moses prayed, and God told him, "'Make a snake and put it up on a pole; anyone who is bitten can look at it and live'" (Numbers 21:8).

A snake on a pole to cure snakebite.

What kind of sense does that make? Who in their right mind would believe that just looking at a fake snake hanging on a pole would work as an antivenom?

But Moses did it. He had a bronze snake fashioned on a pole, and had it erected somewhere in the camp where it could be easily seen. And it worked. Anyone who was bitten by a snake just had to look at the bronze snake-on-a-stick, and they would be healed.

It is a strange story, to be sure.

But the bronze serpent in the wilderness apparently had a purpose. God has a knack for saving and healing stubborn people by seemingly ridiculous methods.

God told Joshua to conquer Jericho by marching his army around the city for six days, without firing a shot, and then, to do so seven times on the seventh day, and to finish by blowing trumpets and shouting loudly. Sounds silly, doesn't it? But Joshua did it, and the walls of Jericho fell.

God's prophet Elisha told a Syrian army commander, a leper named Naaman, to immerse himself seven times in the Jordan River. Crazy, right? But Naaman obeyed and was healed.

It is almost as if God did such things to prepare his people. To build to a crescendo, so to speak. To get them ready for the craziest plan of all.

Jesus told the Pharisee, Nicodemus:

> "Just as Moses lifted up the snake in the wilderness, so the Son of Man must be lifted up, that everyone who believes may have eternal life in him.
>
> "For God so loved the world that he gave his one and only Son, that whoever believes in him shall not perish but have eternal life. For God did not send his Son into the world to condemn the world, but to save the world through him" (John 3:14–17).

Nicodemus didn't quite get what Jesus was saying. Even Jesus' closest friends and followers didn't comprehend—until later, after Jesus was tried and condemned. After he was beaten and made to carry his own cross to the place of execution, a site called Golgotha. After he was nailed to the cross and then lifted up like the snake in the wilderness. After that, they began to understand. The bronze snake prefigured Jesus—the ultimate sacrifice.

Who could have guessed that God's plan for the salvation of the world involved a grueling, brutal death on a cross? Who could have foreseen that as the bronze serpent was raised up in the wilderness, so Jesus would be lifted up on a cross, on a hill called Calvary? Who could have imagined that, just as the ancient Israelites were healed by looking to the serpent, so sinful souls would be saved by turning their eyes on the crucified Jesus and looking to him for forgiveness and cleansing?

It was just the sort of thing God would do. Not only was it unexpected, but counter-intuitive. It is also a fulfillment of the strange and wonderful promise embedded in the story of the bronze serpent, in which a likeness of something cursed became the means of healing. It was a figure of the Coming Savior who, though he was "holy, blameless, pure, [and] set apart from sinners" (Hebrews 7:26), was "made ... to be sin for us" (2 Corinthians 5:21) and became "a curse for us" (Galatians 3:13), "so that in him we might become the righteousness of God" (2 Corinthians 5:21).

FROM THE BIBLE

When he had received the drink, Jesus said, "It is finished." With that, he bowed his head and gave up his spirit.

Now it was the day of Preparation, and the next day was to be a special Sabbath. Because the Jewish leaders did not want the bodies left on the crosses during the Sabbath, they asked Pilate to have the legs broken and the bodies taken down. The soldiers therefore came and broke the legs of the first man who had been crucified with Jesus, and then those of the other. But when they came to Jesus and found that he was already dead, they did not break his legs. Instead, one of the soldiers pierced Jesus' side with a spear, bringing a sudden flow of blood and water. The man who saw it has given testimony, and his testimony is true. He knows that he tells the truth, and he testifies so that you also may believe. These things happened so that the scripture would be fulfilled: "Not one of his bones will be broken," and, as another scripture says, "They will look on the one they have pierced."
—*John 19:30–37*

"Turn to me and be saved, all you ends of the earth;
   for I am God, and there is no other."
—*Isaiah 45:22*

FROM THE HEART

Lord God, your ways are mysterious. Thank you for the holy, blameless, pure, and sinless Jesus dying on the cross for me—He who was made to be sin for me, and made a curse for me—that in him I might become the righteousness of God. I receive His gift of righteousness and salvation. In Jesus' name, amen.

DID YOU KNOW?
The bronze serpent Moses lifted up in the wilderness was apparently preserved for hundreds of years after God used it to heal the Israelites from snakebites. The Bible says that during the reign of King Hezekiah in Judah, "He broke into pieces the bronze snake Moses had made, for up to that time the Israelites had been burning incense to it. (It was called Nehushtan)" (2 Kings 18:4b). In other words, God's people had turned it into an idol!

EXPERIENCE THE STORY: TURN A CURSE INTO PRAYER
It can be an extremely unpleasant experience to hear someone curse. Today, however, turn that experience into prayer: If you hear someone curse, take a moment to silently thank Jesus for becoming a curse for you so that in him you might become the righteousness of God (Galatians 3:13, 2 Corinthians 5:21).

GO DEEPER
For further study, compare the account of the bronze snake in Numbers 21:4–10 with Jesus' words to Nicodemus in John 3:1–21.

REFLECTION TIME
Take a moment and reflect on the question and the insights below:
- (If you're familiar with the chorus, "Turn Your Eyes Upon Jesus.") How can today's reading enlarge the meaning of that chorus to me?
- Select one of the following parallels between the bronze serpent and Jesus to meditate on:
- They were both "lifted up"
- They were the means to healing and salvation
- In both cases, the likeness of something cursed became the means of healing

IT IS FINISHED

Jesus again pulled himself up to the top of his cross. Again he spoke. "Father," he cried, "into your hands I commit my spirit!" One of the soldiers came around to the front of the cross to take another look. Then he went back and lay down on the rock.

From Jesus' lungs came a final cry: "It is finished!" The body sagged on the cross. Jesus willed himself to die.

A sound went through the air as though a herd of animals had stampeded underground. A fresh breeze expelled its brief breath on the wildflowers.

The earth trembled and a small crack fissured the earth from the west toward the east and split the big rock of execution and went across the road and through the gate of Jerusalem and across the town and through the temple, and it split the big inner veil of the temple from the top to the bottom and went on east and rocked the big wall and split the tombs in the cemetery outside the walls and shook the Cedron and went on to the Dead Sea, leaving fissures in the earth, the rocks, and across the mountains.

The centurion and some of the soldiers jumped to their feet in alarm. They came to the front of the cross and looked at him and at the darkened sky and the crack across the big rock. The centurion bowed his head. "Assuredly," he said to the others, "this man was the Son of God."[8]

That scene, from Jim Bishop's classic book, *The Day Christ Died*, depicts the final moments of Jesus' earthly life. From the Bible, we know that his last words were these: "It is finished" (John 19:30).

They are words rich in meaning.

At Passover every year, a spotless lamb was led into the Temple in Jerusalem and tied to the horns of the altar at "the third hour"— 9 a.m., the time at which Jesus had been led to Calvary and nailed to the cross. At "the ninth hour"—3 p.m.—the Pascal Lamb was killed. As the high priest sacrificed the lamb, he spoke a single word in Hebrew—*Kalah*—signifying the ultimate sacrifice of the day. The word means, "It is finished." Jesus, with his dying breath, identified himself as "Christ, our Passover lamb" (1 Corinthians 5:7).

But there was more going on when Jesus said, "It is finished." For centuries, sinful men and women had come to Jerusalem, bringing "the same sacrifices repeated endlessly year after year" (Hebrews 10:1) to atone for their sins. With his final words, Jesus announced the finished work of atonement, "through the sacrifice of the body of Jesus Christ once for all" (Hebrews 10:10). As a great preacher of a past generation said:

> He has finished all that Justice asked, that the Law demanded; He has finished the mission His Father had confided to His hands; He has finished the grand oblation that was to restore to God's moral government the Glory it had lost in man's apostasy. He has finished all the ancient types, predictions and shadows; He has torn the veil in two, and opened the bright pathway for the sinner to retrace his steps back to Paradise, back to God, and once more feel the warm embrace of his Father's forgiving love.[9]

But there is still more meaning in those words. Recall how the first chapters of the Bible say, "By the seventh day God had finished the work he had been doing; so on the seventh day he rested from all his work" (Genesis 2:2). Thus, when the first man woke from his first night of sleep, it was the Sabbath. There was no work for him to do; it was finished. Adam's task was to accept God's gift of the Sabbath and rest.

So it is with the salvation Jesus offers. It is finished. The work is done. Jesus is the fulfillment of the Sabbath; he is your rest. There is no work left to do. There is nothing to prove. Nothing to earn. No striving. No "try," only "take."

Jesus said, "Come to me, all you who are weary and burdened, and I will give you rest" (Matthew 11:28). Your salvation and sustenance comes, not from what you do, but from what is done. Your task is to accept his gift and rest in it. Wake up to it. Enjoy it. And give thanks for it.

FROM THE BIBLE
"I will refresh the weary and satisfy the faint."
—Jeremiah 31:25

Christ, our Passover lamb, has been sacrificed.
—*1 Corinthians 5:7*

There remains, then, a Sabbath-rest for the people of God; for anyone who enters God's rest also rests from their works, just as God did from his.
—*Hebrews 4:9–10*

For you know the grace of our Lord Jesus Christ, that though he was rich, yet for your sake he became poor, so that you through his poverty might become rich.
—*2 Corinthians 8:9*

FROM THE HEART
Lord Jesus, I praise you for finishing all that Justice asked, all the Law demanded; I praise you for finishing the mission your Father had placed in your hands; I praise you for finishing the grand offering, the final sacrifice; I praise you for finishing all the ancient types, predictions, and shadows, for tearing the veil in two, and opening the bright pathway for me back to Paradise, back to God, and back to the warm embrace of my Father's forgiving love. Amen.

DID YOU KNOW?
Some scholars suggest that the genealogy of Jesus in the Gospel of Matthew summarizes Jesus' ancestry in three sets of fourteen generations for a symbolic purpose. Three sets of fourteen, of course,

are also *six* sets of *seven*, which makes Jesus the *seventh seven*. In the Law of Moses, every *seventh year* was a "Sabbath year," and the year after six sets of seven was the Year of Jubilee, in which all debts were forgiven and all slaves were freed. Thus, Matthew depicts Jesus as the seventh seven; *Jesus is the Year of Jubilee*. As he proclaimed in his synagogue sermon in Nazareth, in him all debts are forgiven and all slaves are freed. Jesus is ultimate rest, the fulfillment of the Sabbath.

EXPERIENCE THE STORY: TAKE A MINI-SABBATH

Sometime today, no matter how rushed or hectic your day may be, take a "mini-Sabbath" of five minutes (or more, if possible) and rest. Lay your head down on your desk, or lay back in a recliner. Or simply stop your work and meditate on the finished work of Christ ... for you.

GO DEEPER

For further study, read John's account of the crucifixion in John 19:17–30, and follow it by reading Hebrews 1:3.

REFLECTION TIME

Take some time to reflect on these questions, and write any responses below:

- Do I truly rest in the finished work of Christ, or do I sometimes think I need to work to earn God's favor?
- What can I do today to accept his gift of salvation, and rest in it? Wake up to it? Enjoy it?

FROM THE BELLY OF THE EARTH

After a long day of teaching and healing and interacting with people, Jesus said to his closest friends and followers, "Let's go across the lake."

They crowded into a fishing boat and cast off from the shore. Jesus settled into the stern of the boat to rest. Soon the sky darkened and the wind increased. The lake began to churn and a squall overtook them. The experienced sailors in the group shouted commands at the others; the boat was in danger of being swamped. Each of them cast anxious glances at Jesus, who still slept in the stern.

Finally, Peter stumbled over. "Teacher, don't you care if we drown?"

Jesus didn't answer Peter's question. He simply stood and lifted his hands. He said, "Quiet! Be still!" And the wind ceased. The waters calmed. The crisis passed.

That incident is recorded in three of the four Gospels in the Bible. It is an indication of Jesus' divine power. It is something else, too.

There was once another man who slept through a mighty storm that endangered the lives of the ship's crew. This man, too, had to be awakened, was accused of indifference in the face of danger, and restored calm by his actions. Modern Bible readers may not recognize the parallel, of course. But there is a good chance that Jesus' contemporaries, steeped as they were in the Scriptures, would have recognized a New Jonah in the story of the storm on the Sea of Galilee.

The parallels between Jonah and Jesus don't stop there. Jonah was sent to prophesy first to the Jews (2 Kings 14:25); only *after* this was he sent to the Gentile population of Nineveh, as Jonah 1:1 records. Similarly, Jesus was "sent only to the lost sheep of Israel" (Matthew 15:24), until later in his ministry, when he spoke of his "other sheep that are not in this flock" (John 10:16, NCV).

Jonah was a prophet from Gath Hepher, an insignificant town in Galilee, just a short distance from Jesus' hometown in Nazareth—another unimportant town of Galilee.

Jonah offered to lay down his life in order to save others (Jonah 1:12), like Jesus, who said, "I lay down my life—only to take it up again. No one takes it from me, but I lay it down of my own accord" (John 10:17b–18a).

Another parallel: Though Jonah knew better, the men in his boat could find no fault in him. After Jonah offered himself to be cast overboard:

> The men did their best to row back to land. But they could not, for the sea grew even wilder than before. Then they cried out to the LORD, "Please, LORD, do not let us die for taking this man's life. Do not hold us accountable for killing an innocent man, for you, LORD, have done as you pleased" (Jonah 1:13–14).

Similarly, of course, as Jesus allowed himself to be arrested, tried, and condemned, the Roman governor, Pilate, tried repeatedly to wash his hands of his part in Jesus' death (John 18:38, 19:4, 19:6).

Jesus himself drew more than one parallel between him and the prophet:

> "This is a wicked generation. It asks for a sign, but none will be given it except the sign of Jonah. For as Jonah was a sign to the Ninevites, so also will the Son of Man be to this generation. ... The men of Nineveh will stand up at the judgment with this generation and condemn it, for they repented at the preaching of Jonah; and now something greater than Jonah is here" (Luke 11:29–32).

The act that most signals Jesus as "something greater than Jonah;" however, is the resurrection. Jesus promised: "For as Jonah was three days and three nights in the belly of a huge fish, so the Son of Man will be three days and three nights in the heart of the earth" (Matthew 12:40).

Jesus evoked the story of Jonah as a promise and prophecy of his resurrection, thus once again showing himself to be the fulfillment of prophecy, the one of whom the Scriptures speak (Luke 24:27), the one who escaped the darkness of the grave, the belly of the earth, to "to open eyes that are blind, to free captives from prison and to release from the dungeon those who sit in darkness" (Isaiah 42:7).

FROM THE BIBLE

Jonah obeyed the word of the LORD and went to Nineveh. Now Nineveh was a very large city; it took three days to go through it. Jonah began by going a day's journey into the city, proclaiming, "Forty more days and Nineveh will be overthrown." The Ninevites believed God. A fast was proclaimed, and all of them, from the greatest to the least, put on sackcloth.
—*Jonah 3:3–5*

"I, the LORD, have called you in righteousness; I will take hold of your hand. I will keep you and will make you to be a covenant for the people and a light for the Gentiles, to open eyes that are blind, to free captives from prison and to release from the dungeon those who sit in darkness."
—*Isaiah 42:6–7*

FROM THE HEART

Lord, you have called me in righteousness; you have taken hold of my hand. Thank You for keeping me by Your power; make me a light to those around me. Use me in your great purpose of opening eyes that are blind, freeing captives from prison, and releasing those who sit in darkness. In Jesus' name, amen.

DID YOU KNOW?

The Sanhedrin, the "supreme court" of Israel, once upbraided Nicodemus (who had sought out Jesus privately) for defending Jesus from their schemes. They said, "Are you from Galilee, too? Look into it, and you will find that a prophet does not come out of Galilee" (John 7:52). Interestingly, they were wrong; the prophet Jonah is identified in 2 Kings 14:25 as coming from Gath Hepher, a town in Galilee, just two miles from Nazareth.

EXPERIENCE THE STORY: MEDITATE ON THE SIGN OF JONAH

Jonah spent three days and three nights in the belly of a huge fish; Jesus rose on the third day. Meditate today on the sign of Jonah and the resurrection of Jesus by looking for the numeral three wherever you go. Each time you see a three, whisper a prayer of thanks or an affirmation, such as, "He is risen!"

GO DEEPER

For further study, read the book of Jonah (it is only four short chapters).

REFLECTION TIME

Reflect on one or more of these questions, and take a few moments to record your responses below:

- Read Jonah 2, which consists of Jonah's prayer from the belly of the fish; look for parallels with Jesus' Passion.
- Do I tend to be quick to repent, like the people of Nineveh … or do I resist, like the people of Jesus' day (Luke 11:29–32)?
- God may not call me to witness to a wicked city like Nineveh, or a wicked generation like that of Jesus' day, but what are some ways I can be a light to those around me today?

THE NEW ISRAEL

What was wrong with the number eleven?

Have you ever wondered about that? After all, following the death, resurrection, and ascension of Jesus, the first chapter of Acts describes the next things Jesus' original followers did:

> Then the apostles returned to Jerusalem from the hill called the Mount of Olives, a Sabbath day's walk from the city. When they arrived, they went upstairs to the room where they were staying. Those present were Peter, John, James and Andrew; Philip and Thomas, Bartholomew and Matthew; James son of Alphaeus and Simon the Zealot, and Judas son of James. ...
>
> [And] Peter stood up among the believers (a group numbering about a hundred and twenty) and said, "Brothers and sisters, the Scripture had to be fulfilled in which the Holy Spirit spoke long ago through David concerning Judas, who served as guide for those who arrested Jesus. He was one of our number and shared in our ministry."
>
> (With the payment he received for his wickedness, Judas bought a field; there he fell headlong, his body burst open and all his intestines spilled out. Everyone in Jerusalem heard about this, so they called that field in their language Akeldama, that is, Field of Blood.)
>
> "For," said Peter, "it is written in the Book of Psalms:
>
> "'May his place be deserted; let there be no one to dwell in it,' and, "'May another take his place of leadership.'
>
> Therefore it is necessary to choose one of the men who have

been with us the whole time the Lord Jesus was living among us, beginning from John's baptism to the time when Jesus was taken up from us. For one of these must become a witness with us of his resurrection."

So they nominated two men: Joseph called Barsabbas (also known as Justus) and Matthias. Then they prayed, "Lord, you know everyone's heart. Show us which of these two you have chosen to take over this apostolic ministry, which Judas left to go where he belongs." Then they cast lots, and the lot fell to Matthias; so he was added to the eleven apostles (Acts 1:12–26).

Sounds reasonable enough. But a curious person might wonder, *why did they need a replacement?* Those eleven guys who were left after Judas hanged himself seemed like a pretty capable group. So they were one short. Is that such a big deal?

As it turns out, yes.

Because Jesus hadn't chosen twelve close followers on a whim. The number *twelve* was important because of what Jesus was doing: He was establishing the New Israel.

Generations earlier, God had chosen the twelve sons of Jacob to form the twelve tribes of Israel. He made a covenant with them, and through them intended to bless all the nations of the earth. They were the fulfillment of his promise to Abraham:

> "I will make you into a great nation, and I will bless you …
> and all peoples on earth will be blessed through you"
> (Genesis 12:2a, 3b).

Jesus, in choosing The Twelve—and his disciples, in selecting Matthias to replace Judas—proclaimed the fulfillment of Jeremiah's prophecy:

> "The days are coming," declares the LORD, "when I will make a new covenant. … "I will put my law in their minds and write it on their hearts.
> I will be their God, and they will be my people.
> No longer will they teach their neighbor, or say to one another, 'Know the LORD,'
> because they will all know me, from the least of them to the

greatest," declares the LORD (Jeremiah 31:31a, 33–34a).

It was the herald of a new day, a new covenant. The church was the New Israel, typified in the twelve apostles, and proclaimed by Peter when he wrote to the church: "You are a chosen people, a royal priesthood, a holy nation, God's special possession, that you may declare the praises of him who called you out of darkness into his wonderful light" (1 Peter 2:9).

Those words, of course, include you, if you have trusted Christ for your salvation. You are the New Israel. You are chosen. Royal. Holy. God's special possession. And you are all those things for a reason: "That you may declare the praises of him who called you out of darkness into his wonderful light."

FROM THE BIBLE

For you are a people holy to the LORD your God. The LORD your God has chosen you out of all the peoples on the face of the earth to be his people, his treasured possession.
—*Deuteronomy 7:6*

I provide water in the wilderness and streams in the wasteland, to give drink to my people, my chosen, the people I formed for myself that they may proclaim my praise.
—*Isaiah 43:20–21*

[He] gave himself for us to redeem us from all wickedness and to purify for himself a people that are his very own, eager to do what is good.
—*Titus 2:14*

FROM THE HEART

Almighty God, help me to claim my full inheritance as part of the New Israel. As one who is chosen. Royal. Holy. Your special possession, that I may declare the praises of You who called me out of darkness into Your wonderful light. In Jesus' name, amen.

DID YOU KNOW?

Some scholars see in the meanings of the names of the twelve sons of Israel a prefigure of Jesus Christ—son of God (Reuben), who has heard humanity's cries (Simeon), and makes possible a joining (Levi) of man and God, is worthy (Judah) of praise, is the righteous Judge (Dan) of the world, assists us in our struggle (Naphtali) against sin, can summon a troop (Gad) or company of angels, is the Source of happiness (Asher), will reward (Issachar) his servants, add (Joseph) abundantly to our joys, and sits at the right hand (Benjamin) of the Father.

EXPERIENCE THE STORY: MEDITATE ON THE NEW ISRAEL

Similar to yesterday's experience, meditate today on the numeral twelve wherever you go. Each time you see that number, remind yourself of your inheritance as a chosen people, a royal priesthood, a holy nation, God's special possession, that you may declare the praises of him who called you out of darkness into his wonderful light.

GO DEEPER

For further study, read the account of Jacob's (Israel's) twelve children in Genesis 29:31–30:24. Read also the summary of Jesus' twelve disciples in Mark 3:13–19.

REFLECTION TIME

Reflect on these questions below:

- What are the ways I can declare the praises of Him who has called me out of darkness into His marvelous light?
- Who is God calling me to declare them to?

THE BRIDEGROOM

Jesus could have chosen any setting for his first miracle. He might have healed a blind man after his inaugural sermon in Nazareth, to illustrate his mission of proclaiming "recovery of sight for the blind" (Luke 4:18). He might have appeared on the Sea of Galilee, walking on the water, to show his divine mastery over all of Creation. Or he might have shown up at a funeral and raised someone from the dead, to preview his own resurrection and establish himself as Lord of Life and Conqueror of Death. But he didn't.

Jesus chose to perform his first miracle at a wedding (John 2:1–11). On that occasion, Jesus saved the day. He prevented his neighbors (or relatives) from embarrassment. He kept the party going. But why was a wedding the site of his first miracle? We don't know, but it may have something to do with Jesus' role as the Bridegroom and the church's identity as his bride.

Roughly eight centuries before the wedding in Cana, God spoke to his people through the prophet Hosea. He promised that there would come a day when:

> I will betroth you to me forever; I will betroth you in righteousness and justice,
> in love and compassion.
> I will betroth you in faithfulness, and you will acknowledge the LORD (Hosea 2:19–20).

Sometime after the miracle in Cana, Jesus' cousin, John the Baptist, was questioned about Jesus' increasing popularity, which had begun to overshadow John and his ministry. John replied:

"I told you, 'I am not the Messiah. I am only here to prepare the way for him.' It is the bridegroom who marries the bride, and the best man is simply glad to stand with him and hear his vows. Therefore, I am filled with joy at his success" (John 3:28–29, NLT).

Jesus is that Bridegroom. In Jesus' day, engagements and weddings were done differently than they are in our day and culture. When a man and a woman were engaged, they were legally and morally bound to each other (to such a degree that the engagement could only be broken by divorce). The engagement might last for a year, sometimes more, often depending on how long it took the bridegroom to make all the arrangements, including paying the money or providing the services that constituted the dowry.

When the first day of the wedding finally arrived, the bride would wait in her parents' house for her bridegroom. At the appropriate time, he would appear, dancing and singing, accompanied by his father, her father, and all the wedding guests. He would come to her and place over her head a fine linen veil, bright and clean. Then he would lead her to the chuppah, the canopy of love, where they would embrace, and then, the wedding completed, the feasting would begin.

And the party would go on ... and on ... and on ... for days, even weeks, depending on the wealth of the bridegroom.

That is a picture of Jesus and his relationship to you, as a member of his bride, the church. His dowry was his own lifeblood. He betrothed himself to you (Hosea 2:19–20). And after his resurrection he ascended to heaven with a promise to return and claim his bride. All that awaits is the moment when, with a sound like the roar of rushing waters and loud peals of thunder, the angels of heaven will shout:

"Hallelujah!
For our Lord God Almighty reigns.
Let us rejoice and be glad and give him glory!
For the wedding of the Lamb has come, and his bride has made herself ready.
Fine linen, bright and clean, was given her to wear."
(Fine linen stands for the righteous acts of God's holy people.)

Then the angel [will say]: "Blessed are those who are invited to the wedding supper of the Lamb!" (Revelation 19:6b–9).

The day is coming when Jesus will come to claim his bride. With him will be all the wedding guests—the very host of heaven. It will be a day like no other, and a party like never before, for his glory and wealth are beyond compare. Until then, the bride waits, sometimes anxiously ... but with the constant awareness that soon the light will dawn and the one who promised will come (Revelation 22:20). And the laughter and joy and feasting and love will be unending. "Amen. Come, Lord Jesus" (Revelation 22:20b).

FROM THE BIBLE

As a bridegroom rejoices over his bride, so will your God rejoice over you.
—*Isaiah 62:5*

I feel a divine jealousy for you, since I betrothed you to one husband, to present you as a pure virgin to Christ.
—*2 Corinthians 11:2, ESV*

They were looking intently up into the sky as he was going, when suddenly two men dressed in white stood beside them. "Men of Galilee," they said, "why do you stand here looking into the sky? This same Jesus, who has been taken from you into heaven, will come back in the same way you have seen him go into heaven."
—*Acts 1:10-11*

FROM THE HEART

Lord Jesus, I await you. I await the day of your blessed return. I await the day when the redemption story finds fulfillment, and the truth, justice, mercy, and love of God reigns supreme in heaven and earth. Come, Lord Jesus. Amen.

DID YOU KNOW?

Perhaps the most expensive dowry recorded in the Bible was the seven years of work the cagey Laban extracted from Jacob for Leah, after which he negotiated another seven for Rachel (Genesis 29:15–30)!

EXPERIENCE THE STORY: WORSHIP IN ANTICIPATION

As you worship tomorrow, try your best to do so in a constant awareness of the coming return of the Bridegroom to claim his Bride—and in anticipation of the joy of that day.

GO DEEPER

For further study, read the account of the wedding at Cana in John 2:1–11.

REFLECTION TIME

Reflect on one or more of these questions, and take a few moments to write your responses below:

- Do I look forward to the Lord's return with joy and excitement? Or something else? Why?
- Leonard Sweet and Frank Viola say, "Those who follow Jesus live in the presence of the future."[10] In what ways is that true for you? How can you make it more real to you?
- What can I do today to better prepare myself and those around me for Jesus' coming?

It is difficult to imagine a greater story than what American journalist, playwright, and novelist Fulton Oursler called "The Greatest Story Ever Told"—the story of Jesus, which spans not only a thirty-three year period in the Roman era, but the entire history of God's people.

If *The Bible 30-Day Experience* has spoken to you and blessed you in some way, please consider one more way to apply the teaching of these weeks and these pages to your life. Consider extending the blessing in one—or more—of these ways (see also "Twelve Ways to Follow Up *The Bible 30-Day Experience*" on the following pages):

1. Invite a friend to join you for church this weekend. You may even offer to give your friend a ride to church. You may invite them to have lunch with you afterward. Or you can simply say, "I've been going to (name of church) and really enjoying it. Would you like to come with me this Sunday?"

2. If you've participated in a small group, consider starting a new group—perhaps inviting neighbors or friends from work who don't have a church of their own—to continue and extend the blessing of *The Bible 30-Day Experience*. Even if you've never facilitated a small group before, you have now been through the experience and know how easy it is to use the small-group discussion guidebook. Information for ordering materials is provided at the back of this book.

3. Brainstorm—perhaps with your pastor or small-group leader—more ways to share *The Bible 30-Day Experience* with others. Whatever you do, don't keep it to yourself.

Let the message about Christ, in all its richness, fill your lives. Teach and counsel each other with all the wisdom he gives. Sing psalms and hymns and spiritual songs to God with thankful hearts. And whatever you do or say, do it as a representative of the Lord Jesus, giving thanks through him to God the Father (Colossians 3:16–17, NLT).

WEEK FIVE: SMALL-GROUP STUDY AND DISCUSSION QUESTIONS

Below is a complete list of small-group study and discussion questions for small groups that use this guidebook in conjunction with *The Bible 30-Day Experience DVD Study*. In order to stay within the time limits of your small-group meeting, your small-group leader will choose what questions he or she wants your group to focus on. You will want to bring this guidebook with you to your small group or class.

1. Open in prayer.

2. Go around the room asking everyone to briefly answer this question: "What is the most amazing thing you've ever experienced or witnessed?"

3. Watch video: "The Early Jerusalem Church"

4. Question: "As you watched the video, which event did you find most miraculous?"

5. Question: "Would the amazing events on the video have seemed less or more realistic if the setting had been the twenty-first century? Why?"

6. Read Acts 2:42–3:10

7. Question: "How is the description of the church's life and activity in Acts 2:42–47 different from the description of Jesus' followers in John 20:19? Why?"

8. Question: "How is the description of the church's life and activity in Acts 2:42–47 similar to your church's life and activity? How is it different?"

9. Question: "Notice that Acts 3:2 specifically mentions that the beggar had been crippled from birth. Why do you think that detail was included?"

10. Question: "Notice what Peter said to the beggar in Acts 3:6. He had never said or done this before. What do you think Peter might have been thinking as he said those words?"

11. Question: "What do you think the crippled beggar sitting

in the shadow of the temple might have been thinking as he heard Peter's words?"

12. Question: "Which do you think shows more faith, Peter commanding the beggar to get up and walk, or the beggar taking Peter's hand to stand up? Why?"

13. Question: "The message theme this past Sunday was 'Journey from Darkness to Light.' How might this passage reflect the idea of God's gracious salvation leading people from darkness into light?"

14. Question: "Do you think the Jerusalem church—and Peter, in particular—had more faith or more power than we do today? Why or why not?"

15. Question: "Do you think there are ways your church—and you, in particular—should be or can be more like these verses? If not, why not? If so, how?"

16. Any other questions or comments?

17. Close in prayer.

TWELVE WAYS TO FOLLOW UP
THE BIBLE 30-DAY EXPERIENCE

While the Week Five "Weekly Review" suggested a few ways to extend the blessing of *The Bible 30-Day Experience*, there is no good reason to limit yourself to those suggestions. So, if you have benefitted from these past thirty days, here are twelve more ways to follow up *The Bible 30-Day Experience*:

1. Start the experience all over again as a personal study, using this guidebook and other materials from the series to further review, deepen, and experience the things you've learned.

2. Repeat the experience with your small group—only this time, invite others who weren't a part of the experience the first time (neighbors, family members, etc.) to join in.

3. Spin off one or more new small groups from your group to include people who missed out the first time through. See "How to Start a New Small Group" on the following pages for helpful suggestions.

4. If there were some resources you didn't explore the first time through *The Bible 30-Day Experience* (such as the companion novel, devotional, etc.), this would be a great time to use them as follow-up resources. These are available at Outreach.com/Bible.

5. Read further in some of the resources mentioned in this book, such as Jim Bishop's *The Day Christ Died* or *Jesus: A Theography* by Leonard Sweet and Frank Viola.

6. Begin a one-on-one discipleship program using *The Bible 30-Day Experience* materials as your curriculum (see "How to Start a One-on-One Discipling Relationship" on the following pages for guidance).

7. Host a study at your workplace, community hall, neighborhood coffee shop, etc., to expose new people to the life-changing impact of *The Bible 30-Day Experience*.

8. Obtain the entire home entertainment DVD of *The Bible* and

view the whole miniseries again, watching for new types of Christ and figures of salvation in the stories.

9. Once you have the home entertainment DVD of *The Bible*, consider starting Home Viewing Parties as an outreach to friends, family, and co-workers. Each week, together you can watch an episode and then discuss what you've watched, experienced, and learned. To get a Home Viewing Party Kit contact Outreach at (800) 991-6011 or visit Outreach.com/Bible.

10. Your church could host a public viewing where the congregation and the community are invited to come and experience the entire miniseries of the Bible. New small groups could launch in conjunction with this public viewing, so that people could ask questions and learn more about how the Bible applies to their lives. To find out more about how your church can obtain a site license for public viewing, please contact Outreach at (800) 991-6011 or visit Outreach.com/Bible.

11. Suggest a new study experience to your pastor or group leader, perhaps choosing from one of the resources listed in the back of this book.

12. Get together with others—perhaps your pastor or small group leader—and brainstorm other ways to share *The Bible 30-Day Experience* with others.

HOW TO START A NEW SMALL GROUP

Starting—and facilitating—a small group is not a difficult process, especially with a resource like *The Bible 30-Day Experience DVD Study*. Here are a few suggestions to get you started, even if you've never led a group before:

Check with your pastor or church leadership. There may already be a process in place or training opportunities and guidelines available through your church.

Draw up a list of people to invite to join the small group. This is another good reason to check with your church's leadership, as you'll want to invite people who aren't already involved in a small group.

Decide on a regular day, time, and place for your small group to meet. While some groups enjoy rotating locations, it's probably best to begin with a set time and place. It is also best to meet weekly, especially for the duration of *The Bible 30-Day Experience.*

Decide how large you want the group to be. Generally speaking, a group of ten or twelve in regular attendance is the maximum size to allow for open discussion and provides great opportunities for study and relationship building.

Set a date and place for a "kick off" meeting. This should occur at the same day, time, and place you plan for subsequent meetings.

Issue invitations through the mail or e-mail, and follow up with a phone call or "in person" invitation. Depending on how well you know the people on your list, you may want to invite two or three times the anticipated size of your group, since there will certainly be some who are unable to accept your invitation for any number of reasons.

At your "kick off" meeting, provide light refreshments, introduce the study, and distribute resources, such as this guidebook. Before ending the meeting, make sure everyone knows where and when the next meeting will take place.

Follow the small-group discussion notes in this guidebook for each subsequent meeting. Encourage participants to make the most of the daily readings and weekly reviews.

Toward the end of the five-week study, encourage group members to consider launching more small groups themselves, thus extending The Bible 30-Day Experience.

HOW TO START A ONE-ON-ONE
DISCIPLING RELATIONSHIP

You do not have to be a spiritual giant in order to mentor someone else in the faith, especially when a resource like *The Bible 30-Day Experience DVD Study* is available. Here are a few tips to help you get started:

Identify someone you would like to bless and help to grow spiritually. This should be someone of the same sex who has not yet experienced *The Bible 30-Day Experience.*

Begin praying regularly for that person. Ask God to open or close the door to a discipling relationship, as he chooses.

Approach that person. Whether in writing, on the phone, or in person, approach the person you've been praying for and ask if he or she would like to meet with you six times over five weeks (an initial meeting followed by five weekly meetings) to learn and grow spiritually. If he or she responds positively, move on to the next step; if he or she isn't sure or declines, be patient. Simply suggest, "Let me know if you change your mind," and begin praying for God to change that person's mind or suggest someone new to you.

Set a regular day, time, and place to meet. Collaborate on choosing a time and place that works for both of you to meet weekly for the duration of *The Bible 30-Day Experience.*

Make your first meeting a "get better acquainted" time. Give your companion a copy of this guidebook. You may also want to bring a Bible to give away, if there's a chance he or she doesn't own one. Explain how to use the guidebook's daily readings and weekly reviews prior to your next meeting.

Adapt the small-group studies for use as a guide for your one-on-one discussions. Note: if possible, plan to meet in a private place with access to a DVD player to facilitate the viewing of each video in the weekly study.

When you complete the five weeks of *The Bible 30-Day Experience*, encourage your companion to begin meeting with someone else, with whom *they* can share the experience. Assure them that you will remain available to coach and guide them as they establish a new one-on-one discipling relationship.

Start the process anew, by praying for the next person you would like to bless and help to grow spiritually.

NOTES

1. A. W. Tozer, The Tozer Pulpit, Vol. 2 (Camp Hill, PA: Christian Publications, 1994), 127.

2. R. C. Sproul, Romans: The Righteous Shall Live By Faith (Wheaton, IL: Crossway Books, 2009), 296.

3. Matthew Henry, Matthew Henry's Concise Commentary on the Whole Bible (Nashville: Thomas Nelson Publishers, 1997), 89.

4. Dante Alighieri, The Divine Comedy (New York: Oxford University Press, 2008), 390.

5. "Ancient Seal May Add Substance to the Legend of Samson," Science Daily, August 13, 2012.

6. Leonard Sweet and Frank Viola, Jesus: A Theography (Nashville: Thomas Nelson Publishers, 2012), 283–284.

7. Matthew Henry, Matthew Henry's Complete Commentary on the Whole Bible, commentary on Daniel 6:1 (http://www.studylight.org/com/mhm/view.cgi?book=da&chapter=006), 1706.

8. Jim Bishop, The Day Christ Died (New York: Harper and Brothers, 1957), 308.

9. From a sermon delivered on Thursday, April 4, 1861, as found at http://www.ccel.org/ccel/spurgeon/sermons07.xxx.html

10. Leonard Sweet and Frank Viola, Jesus: A Theography (Nashville: Thomas Nelson Publishers, 2012), 286.

EXPERIENCE THE BIBLE LIKE NEVER BEFORE!

The *Bible 30-Day Experience DVD-Based Study* is a five-week study based on some of the epic stories of the Bible, with an emphasis on God's plan for the redemption of mankind through Jesus Christ. This study features inspirational video clips from *The Bible*, an epic miniseries that originally aired on the History Channel. It also includes *The Bible 30-Day Experience Guidebook*, which contains thirty lessons and daily readings on the foreshadowing of Jesus in the stories of the Bible, along with pertinent Scriptures, small-group study and discussion questions, and weekly message overviews.

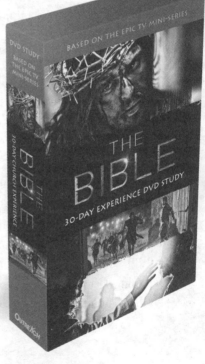

This series will help participants to:

1. See these epic stories from the Bible like they never have before.
2. Discover the scarlet thread of redemption through Jesus Christ woven throughout the Bible.
3. Experience a greater insight into God's amazing love for them personally.
4. Understand how their story fits within God's overarching story for all of us.
5. Be inspired to read these great stories from God's Word themselves.

The *Bible 30-Day Experience DVD-Based Study Kit* is available online or at your local Christian bookstore. Bulk quantities available at Outreach.com/Bible.